Who's afraid of Donald Trump?

And Other Politically Incorrect Essays

By Justin Southworth

Table of Contents

Part One: Who's Afraid of Donald Trump?

INTRODUCTION

The campaign and presidency of Donald Trump, even this early in his administration, is the most divisive phenomena in my personal memory, reaching back to JFK. The criticism of the man is more than vituperative and more than cruel. It demonstrates a hatred of the man and everything he represents unprecedented in modern politics. What is it about the person of Donald John Trump that breeds such virulent hostility toward him? Competing *weltanschauungs* among factions within The United States of America are currently driving a struggle for legitimacy and power with such intensity and go-for-broke aggressiveness as hasn't been seen since the 1850s. This man Trump is referred to by his detractors as a misogynist, racist, homophobic, anti-Jewish, demagogue. Those are only the milder epithets hurled at him. One doesn't have to search too diligently to find him referred to as demagoguing bag of candy corn, muddled asshole yearning to scream free, crotch-fondling slab of rancid meatloaf, screaming carrot demon, the asteroid that just destroyed a party of dinosaurs, inside-out lower intestine, man-sized sebaceous cyst, bag of toxic sludge, human turd, and a dusty barrel of fermented peepee. Those are just a small sample of the phrases I can write in a book without age restrictions. The list could go on and on with countless more, but you get the point.

And why?

> Is Mr. Trump a homophobe? No.
> A racist? No.
> A misogynist? No.
> Anti-Jewish? No.
> Anti-Mexican or Xenophobic? No.
> An idiot? Far from it.

What Mr. Trump is not, at least not as of the date of this writing, is a politician. (Unfortunately, he will become one or he will not survive his term in office.) *Dave* was a popular movie from 1990. Supposedly this spoke to tens of millions of Americans who were tired of professional politicians. In this movie, Americans truly wanted a down-to-earth everyman in the office of president. Frank Capra's *Mr. Smith Goes to Washington* is an example of the same sentiment from eighty years ago. The mythology that has accrued to "Honest Abe Lincoln" speaks to the same sentiment and gives credence to the idea that Americans, deep down, want, or at least *think* they want, a humble, sincere, civil servant as chief executive of the government. But as much as the general populace says they want an honest, down-to-earth common man for president, someone who understands Middle America, someone who will simply say what he's thinking and will be honest with the voters, when someone with those qualities appears he is trashed for speaking his unfiltered mind.

The vitriol from his detractors doesn't stop at the president. No, it is extended to everyone who might not hate him as much as those who occupy the Cultural Marxist, Social Justice Warrior (SJW) class of snowflakes who conjure up the epithets and vitriol above. Anyone who is not with them is one of the *deplorables* identified by Ms. Clinton—those in fly-over country without Ivy League law degrees who work and care for families as Americans did in decades past, those from homes with old fashioned male and female parents, who think it's not such a bad idea to put America's interests first in foreign and economic policy, who think handing out welfare checks to illegal immigrants is not a good idea, who still attend church and unashamedly value our Judeo-Christian heritage.

So let's take a look at the screeds thrown at Mr. Trump that began at the point in his campaign for the presidency where it seemed he might actually be a contender. Prior to that time, barbs against him were more jocular. The press took his candidacy as nothing more than a publicity stunt. Its value was purely in the entertainment provided by his persona. But the day it became apparent that he actually had a chance to win the Republican nomination, the rhetoric of fear and loathing began. With every passing day, the mainstream press reporting became more hateful, vile, and vituperative. By the time the primaries were over and the campaigns of the two major party nominees were well underway, it was apparent to anyone who was paying attention that ninety percent of the mainstream press was solidly, unreservedly, and unabashedly in the camp of Hillary Rodham Clinton. The well-scripted and rehearsed screeds and talking points came fast and furious from virtually every source of "news" media. Mr. Trump was obviously not groomed as a politician, nor even as a public speaker. He didn't read from a script. He hadn't had the decades of experience of rising through the political ranks where one learns to carefully consider and weigh each and every word for each and every possible hidden meaning that a far left-leaning liberal media might misconstrue.

America today is gripped in the vice of political correctness run amuck. In effect, the mantra of *Thou Shalt Not Offend* has become our national motto and is virtually the first commandment of our national religion of inclusiveness and tolerance (of everyone except conservatives). Indeed, the previous motto, *In God we Trust,* is now anathema to the SJW's among us. And we as a people have become so sensitive that we search through each individual's speech, actions, and thoughts, to the extent we are able to imagine them, for *micro*-aggressions and *micro*-offenses. These micro-aggressions and offenses are not based on any objective reality, but are purely situational and seen completely in relation to the perceiver's own sense of Fairness and Social Justice, however warped, subjective, and unreasonable it may be. The same sentiments felt and the same words spoken by a "person of color" and a "colorless person" are interpreted completely independently and normally opposite of each other. An organization with the name *La Raza* (Spanish for The Race), whose purpose is the promotion of causes of particular interest to Hispanic people is perfectly acceptable. An organization called *The Race* (in English), on the other hand, whose basis might be the promotion of causes of particular interest to people of European descent would be pilloried by one and all within the narrow confines of the self-described *Intelligencia* as bigoted and racist.

Until Mr. Trump, those who reached the level of American politics where they might mount a credible campaign for the presidency would have been groomed for decades for that position. But we have come to a sea change in America; a good portion of the populace, the *deplorables*, have reached the end of our collective patience. We do not want more of the same, and more of the same is exactly who the Democratic Party put forward for their standard bearer. In fact, Hillary Clinton was not just more of the same, but the next level of the result of decades spent in a pursuit of the bottom of the political barrel. Half of the American voters believe this woman to be the very embodiment of the most vile, corrupt, manipulative, dishonest, power-hungry traits anyone might possibly imagine inhabiting a single human being. Millions of people considered Donald Trump and did not see the ideal presidential candidate, but they did see someone whom they believed to be at least somewhat open and honest in his speech and had sincere concern for everyman, not just the bankers and relatively tiny cadre of the powerful who pull the strings of control. These people knew he was the product of a ruthless, competitive business environment, that he was a man who grew up in an America before micro-aggression was even a word. His words are not always polite. In fact, he can be crude and rude, but to be otherwise in the cut-throat business world of New York is to be a failure. If there is one thing no one can say of the man, it is that he is a failure in any sense of the word.

However, after a century of government-provided education, Americans distrust the world of business. We see those who make a career of politics, those whose livelihoods depend upon the state, *that entity that controls a geographical space and derives its power purely through the threat or use of violence*, as somehow morally superior to those who derive their livelihood by offering products and services in an environment of voluntary exchange. One might wonder how the people of a nation that grew from nothing more than the germ of an idea to the economic powerhouse of the world in less than two centuries based on the simple concepts of respect for property and free enterprise can have thrown off such a prosperous tradition so easily and so quickly.

The answer is clear. Who controls education controls the minds of the populace. This is from *The Holocaust*

Explained,[1] a web site directed at children, but accurate and simple:

> *Controlling education was a way of taking over the minds of children from kindergarten to university. Education was a major tool by which the Nazis' racial policies were promoted and implemented.*
>
> *Initially, many teachers ignored the political changes. However, very soon, those German teachers who supported the Nazis or had been converted to Nazism began to develop new daily rituals and routines. Many of the 32 per cent of teachers who became Nazi Party members would wear their uniform to school.*
>
> *All teachers had to swear an oath of allegiance to Hitler and teach in accordance with Nazi ideas and values. All Jewish teachers were dismissed, as were teachers who refused to support the Nazi Party's ideals.*
>
> *The atmosphere within the classroom was very different from the one students had known previously. The teacher would enter the classroom and welcome the group with a 'Hitler salute', shouting "Heil Hitler!" Students would have to respond in the same manner, often eight times each day – at the start and end of the day, as well as the beginning and end of each lesson.*

The United States Department of Education differs in degree, but not in principle. Books used in government

---

[1] http://www.theholocaustexplained.org/ks3/life-in-nazi-occupied-europe/controlling-everyday-life/controlling-education/#.WNFZJjsrKUk

schools must be stringently vetted and approved by federal and state government agencies or school boards that are extremely influenced by those agencies. The *Heil Hitler* raised-hand salute was replaced by the daily Pledge of Allegiance and the hand over the heart. (In fact, the raised hand salute in America was only replaced after it became associated with Hitler and Nazi Germany.) An honest appraisal of the U.S. government's manipulation of other countries' economics and politics will never be allowed in the public schools. An honest assessment of the causes of the Great Depression is left to the very few who care to delve into the subject after their high school years. [2] American students are taught of the evils of the "robber barons" and the goodness of government programs that built the Trans-continental Railroad, ignoring the dramatic reduction in costs of shipping brought about by those "barons," ignoring the financial success of the Great Northern Railroad, built without government help, and ignoring the ruinous costs and decades of repair and re-routing of the Trans-continental Railroad due to shoddy workmanship and bad routing, both the direct result of government incentives designed for the financial benefit of congress-critters and their cronies in business and industry. Students will never hear of the political, economic, and human disaster brought upon Europe as a result of U.S. involvement in World War One, of the war crimes perpetrated by the U.S. in the Philippines after the contrived Spanish-American War, or the Hawaiian side of the conquest of those islands by the U.S. at the end of the nineteenth century. In short, American students learn a lopsided and in many ways dishonest version of U.S. and world history, to say nothing of left-leaning social justice agenda they are fed year after year with a "Government

---

[2] For example, see *America's Great Depression* by Murray Rothbard. Details in the bibliography.

Good/Business Bad" theme running right through the middle.

W.J. Astore quotes Christian Bay in his article, "Yes. Education is About Social Control."[3]

> *Education in my sense of liberating and strengthening (making articulate and uncompromising) the intellect is of course antithetical to much of what is going on in our schools and universities, which I would rather refer to by such terms as training, molding, socialization, mystification, memorizing of facts, obfuscation of meaning—all processes designed to produce intelligent citizens who are ready to execute jobs faithfully and not ask any questions about their meaning or purpose or value to fellow human beings.*
>
> *Education today still largely teaches students to stay within their station. Today's focus on vocational education is both salutary and one-dimensional. Students are told to get degrees as passports to a job. They're not told to aspire to be skeptical citizens who dare to question (or even to supplant) authority.*

And there we have it—generations of Americans who have been instilled with the Stockholm Complex. We not only trust and obey our masters, but we grow to respect and love them. If there be any skepticism, it is easily overcome by the mainstream media that are controlled by the same people at the bottom of the rat holes down which we pour the wealth of the nation to be consumed by the *One*

---

3 https://contraryperspective.com/2013/07/14/yes-education-is-about-social-control/

Percenters of the military-congressional-industrial complex at the bottom.

The American government, in the middle of the second decade of the twenty-first century, is nearing successful implementation of Saul Alinsky's eight rules for radicals with institutions and programs that allow the complete control of an ignorant populace by the elites in government:

1) Healthcare – Control healthcare and you control the people.
2) Poverty – Increase the poverty level as high as possible; poor people are easier to control and will not fight back if you are providing everything for them to live.
3) Debt – Increase the debt to an unsustainable level. That way you are able to increase taxes and this will produce more poverty.
4) Gun control – Remove people's ability to defend themselves from the government. That way you are able to create a police state.
5) Welfare – Take control of every aspect of people's lives (food, housing and income).
6) Education – Take control of what people read and listen to; take control of what children learn in school.
7) Religion – Remove the belief in God from the government and schools.
8) Class warfare – Divide the people into the wealthy and the poor. This will cause more discontent and it will be easier to take from *(tax)* the wealthy with the support of the poor.

Given a frightened populace easily controlled by selective dissemination of "news" in the mainstream media, the tiny oligarchy in control of the government of the United States is able to promote any ideas it desires about Mr. Trump and to *misdirect* the attention of the people from matters that will affect the survival of this country in any guise its founders envisioned. This is all for the benefit of the Deep State, aided and abetted by *useful idiots*.

This is not to say that Mr. Trump does not have serious flaws and may make serious errors in his position as president. But those issues are too complex for the education level of the general populace, so to address them is a waste of print space and air time. His flaws comprise exactly the same qualities of hubris, a decidedly narrow worldview, and blustering Americanism as his principal opponent in the campaign for president, so of course these issues cannot be brought out and debated without blowing the lid off the whole sordid political game played by national politicians and their media enablers.

With that said, the power-brokers do not believe they can impose the controls over Mr. Trump they feel are necessary to achieve their goals of a New World Order. The goal of the Deep State is to remove him from office. The easiest and fastest route to that end is through a number of insignificant issues that can be wrapped up with a bow and presented to an American hyper sensitive populace more in tune with the progress of contestants on *The Voice* than with issues relevant to the continuance of the human race and individual liberty. Only the most mundane, trivial, and fleeting issues can be presented to the majority of Americans as reasons to disqualify Mr. Trump from office. These are presented *ad nauseum* as never-ending screeds. As of the time of this writing, these criticisms have begun to leave the pages of the "respectable" mainstream media, but are carried on by tabloid journalism. Regardless, the criticisms have done their job; they followed Mr. Trump as he entered office as a foul smelling trail of offal. He took his seat in the Oval Office already at the bottom of the ninth with two strikes against him.

If Donald Trump's presidency survives four years, given what he has had to endure during the campaign and only a few months into his term, he should be counted as one of America's most talented and intelligent presidents.

The Screeds

Screed: *a ranting piece of writing, a long and often angry piece of writing that usually accuses someone of something or complains about something.* (from *Merriam-Webster Online Dictionary*)

SCREED NUMBER ONE: DONALD TRUMP IS HOMOPHOBIC

Homophobic: *irrational fear of, aversion to homosexuality or homosexuals* (Merriam-Webster Online Dictionary)

Should anyone who desires to have sexual relations with another living human being over a (socially acceptable and/or legal) minimum age fear Donald Trump?

That's a round-about way of trying to include any and all sexual orientations and identifications which seem to grow in number daily. By this I include heterosexual, non-heterosexual, gray asexual, homosexual, bisexual, asexual, androgynous, pansexual, polysexual, gender binary, transgender, sysgender, gender-neutral, gender-fluid, queer, change-your-mind-from-day-to-day depending on barometric pressure or any other factor, identifiable or not, and any other manner in which one wants to define oneself based on whom one prefers to have or not have sex with. I include the qualifiers living, human, and of legal age in the first sentence of this section to narrow the universe of possible sexual partners; as of this writing, we're not at the point where we're claiming the right to have sexual relations with non-living humans, animals, or children as a civil right. That, I fear, is only a matter of time. No doubt, I'll have to update this paragraph when the second edition is published.

What, exactly, is the LGBTQIAPK etc, etc, etc. community afraid of?

According to Charles Moran, a noted gay Republican,[4] "Donald Trump is the best candidate that the LGBT community has ever seen come out of the Republican Party." (We can assume he meant to include QIAPK etc, etc, etc.) Detractors will jump on the "Republican Party" qualifier, but Mr. Trump has stated that the Supreme Court decisions on gay marriage are in the past and the law is settled. When asked about his opinion on same sex marriage, he said he's "fine with that." He has gone so far as to suggest that he would *not* try to nominate judges for the purpose of overturning gay marriage decisions. So the man the Left has equated with Hitler and has been literally called a Nazi says he's fine with gay marriage. Asked about the "bathroom issue," he tossed it away with the comment that transgender people should use whatever bathroom they're comfortable with. This from a man who doesn't weigh every word he says, as if reading a script. He says exactly what he thinks. Mr. Trump was the first Republican nominee to mention the LGBTQ community in an acceptance speech. "As your president, I will do everything in my power to protect our LGBTQ citizens from the violence and oppression of a hateful foreign ideology. Believe me."

Talk is cheap, though, so how are we to know whether Mr. Trump was just pandering? The Don may not have a political history to judge by, but he has a long and significant history of business dealings. He ensured there was no prohibition or any sort of discrimination against gay members of his Mar-a-Lago Country Club. He publicly

---

4 (http://abcnews.go.com/Politics/gay-republicans-explain-proudly-supporting-donald-trump/story?id=42977880)

gave his support for the marriage of Elton John to David Furnish. If nothing else, Donald Trump is a realist; being anti-gay is bad for business and it's bad politics. Therefore, he is not.

What they're afraid of, methinks, is that Mr. Trump has taken away the power of the militant LGBTQIAPK (etc, etc, etc.) community to complain about a political leader who is to the right of center, if only very slightly, and, heaven forbid, a registered Republican. That, they cannot have. Juan Hernandez, quoted in the same story noted above, said, "This has been the most inclusive president[ial candidate] that we've had in the Republican Party and it is so exciting that the movement is here." Hernandez speaks not only as a gay supporter of Mr. Trump, but as a Hispanic as well. Mr. Hernandez has suffered for his beliefs—physically. He was beaten by an anti-Trump protestor at a Trump campaign rally in San Jose, California. The attack left him with a broken nose and the "realization that supporting his candidate in the mostly liberal Bay Area can be dangerous." So much for "love trumps hate."

Mr. Moran says, "...it's so much easier to be gay in the Republican Party than it is to be a Republican in the LGBT community." Whence the vitriol comes directed at Mr. Trump from the LGBTQIAPK etc., etc., etc. community? Could it be that their leadership feels they have to keep the rank and file in a high state of alert in order to seem relevant? To continue the fear necessary to maintain the financial contributions to the various organizations that support the LGBTQIAPK etc., etc., etc. community? Any organization's prime motive is survival, and survival by any means necessary, even if those means include lying, misdirecting, and outright deceiving its own gullible members.

We can safely say Mr. Trump's presidency will bring no harm to the community of persons who identify themselves according to whom they prefer to have or not have sexual relations with.

Mr. Trump is not homophobic in any sense of the word.

Misogynistic, from misogyny: *a hatred of women.* (Merriam-Webster Online Dictionary)

President Trump has employed many women in management positions within his businesses and presidential campaign staff, and appointed the first woman as Surgeon General, Rear Adm. Sylvia Trent-Adams. Misogynist? That's hard for me to believe. And from the evidence presented below, this would seem on its face to be a ludicrous accusation; obviously, Mr. Trump likes women very much.

All facetiousness aside, we know what his accusers mean: that Mr. Trump "objectifies" women; he observes at a woman, notes her outer attractiveness, and, if appealing, his genetic programming tells him to make a move on her. It seems several times throughout his life he has taken action upon this programming.

After eons of human existence where this was the norm, we have, in the last couple of decades, come to the realization that male assertiveness, or non-violent aggressiveness toward women is, in fact, evidence of the subject's closeted *hatred* of womankind, of misogyny. The left-liberal progressives among us have redefined this type of behavior from simply boorish and, in some circumstances, socially unacceptable to misogynistic. In fact, that relatively small group of *cognoscenti*, in Orwellian fashion, change the definition of words seemingly at random. Or maybe I should say, *Carrollian* fashion[5]: *"When I use a word,"* Humpty Dumpty said, in rather a scornful tone, *"it means just what I choose it to mean—neither more nor less."* The word boorish has no

---

[5] Lewis Carroll. *Through the Looking-Glass*

emotional appeal, so Mr. Trump, according to the Humpty Dumpties of the world, is now misogynistic. Progressives enjoy co-opting words with strong emotional appeal. These days, a misogynist is anyone who looks at a woman "with lust in his heart,"[6] or who even sees any woman as attractive by purely visual references, as in, before he's met her, spoken with her, and discovered *her true inner (BBW?) beauty.*

To the realists and adult-minded this is problematic: Before one can get to know another person, visual contact is, in the vast majority of cases, the first experience two people share. As stated above, the prime objective of an organism (or organization) is survival. Life wants to beget life, to continue the species. God, or Nature, or nature if you prefer, has given all living beings an innate ability to detect partners most likely to carry on the species. Among these, at least in mammals (I cannot speak about fish, birds, or things that crawl upon the Earth) are a healthy body (not too thin, not too fat), clear skin, symmetrical facial features, healthy hair (beautiful, flowing locks), and healthy teeth (a great smile and pleasant breath, an indicator of health). Women have their own set of criteria for choosing mates for their purposes. Genetic programming for most women, just as for men, creates a desire for a mate who can procreate and produce healthy offspring. This is demonstrated by a healthy dose of testosterone, of which evidence is a tall, muscular frame with facial hair and a low, resonant voice. In decades and centuries past, the physical ability to provide for her and her children and to be able to protect them from physical

---

6 President Jimmy Carter admitted to two Playboy freelance writers that he had "looked on a lot of women with lust" and had "committed adultery in my heart many times." Thus President Carter, in today's parlance, would be a misogynist.

danger was the prime characteristic desired. In modern society, physical prowess has given way, when practical matters are considered, to the ability to earn money. In fact, some will say the aforementioned physical qualities are no longer necessary, that a man doesn't have to physically protect his mate and that other psychic and emotional qualities are much more important to a long-term relationship. But a million years of instinct imprinted in our DNA is not overcome in the relatively short period in which was developed capitalism and the division of labor that rewards mental acuity more than physical. We still have incredibly strong instincts that drive our conscious and subconscious choices, and those choices are still determined by a healthy appearance, an appearance we have come to regard as "beautiful."

Say what you will about the ability or right of women to "have it all," but the fact remains that during child rearing years a woman and her children are much better off with a male partner who has the talent and knowledge to provide a safe, secure home well-suited to the rearing of children and for keeping the vicissitudes of life on the other side of the walls.

As long as we're talking about sex, let's get right to the accusations of Mr. Trump's sexual predations. By any honest reckoning, there have been many accusations. The fact that many of them, stemming from supposed behavior of many years ago, only came to light during the last year of Mr. Trump's campaign for president will go without analysis. The fact that some accusers were found to be closely associated with the campaign of his principal (female) opponent will also get a pass. At the time of this writing, very early in Mr. Trump's presidency, I don't know of a case that has been adjudicated against him.

The best known of Mr. Trump's *faux pas* took place on a corporate bus en route to a television studio in September of 2005 and was recorded by William Hall "Billy" Bush, a radio and television host and member of the Bush family that produced, so far, two presidents, a family who have never tried to hide their hatred and rancor toward the new president. The surreptitious recording of a conversation between Mr. Bush and Mr. Trump caught the celebrity (not candidate at that time) saying some off-color things about some of the women he'd met in "show business." His now famous quote is, "They let you do it. You can do anything. Grab them by the pussy. You can do anything."

His supporters' claim that was just locker-room talk. I can't honestly vouch for that. I've been in plenty of high school, college, and health club locker rooms and never heard anything closely resembling what is commonly referred to as "locker room talk." With that said, I've never been in a locker room full of high-achieving, powerful men who, as a matter of course, run rich on testosterone and possibly do say that kind of thing among compatriots. I have been in hunting cabins with men, after a day in the cold woods, sitting by a fire with a cigar in one hand and a bottle of beer in another, whose talk has approached that. I also believe Donald Trump when he says Bill Clinton has said worse on the golf course, but that's a subject for a different day. Mr. Trump's language is nothing more nor less crude than that of the normal man raised in the Brooklyn of the 60's and 70's. We, accustomed to political correctness and fearful of *micro-aggressions*, may find his manner of speaking crude, but this is the language of the men of his generation in the environs of New York City. Mr. Trump is not a life-long politician, taught to speak only after every word has been parsed and weighed and carefully considered for its alternative meanings, pondering how every phrase might be heard, interpreted, and then reported by a hostile news media. His brash talk, off-the-cuff honesty, and bull-in-a-china shop personality are exactly what has enabled him to build the business empire he has. The man isn't erudite, but when he speaks the majority of Americans know what he is saying, and what he is saying is what he is feeling. No holds barred. Good or bad, they appreciate his frankness and honesty.

Let's review a couple of facts though, with openness and honesty.

What I've picked up in my sixty years on Earth is that many people in the entertainment industry are indeed somewhat willing to "go the extra mile" with a well-known, powerful personality, regardless of whether that person be someone normally in front of or behind the camera. You can't throw a rock in Los Angeles without hitting a beautiful, talented, wanna-be actor (we used to say actress, but that's un-PC. I trust you know I'm talking mostly, but not solely, about female actors.) Not always, but certainly not rarely, some powerful, male, testosterone-rich producer, director, or A-list star (male actor, normally, but not exclusively) will expect a little extra from an auditionee in order to be noticed. Out of the million or so talented, beautiful female actors, there are many, if we can be honest, who will in fact allow themselves to be "grabbed by the pussy." Is it right or just to condemn Mr. Trump for commenting on this?

If you listen to the interview you'll note that he didn't say he, personally *did* grab anyone, he said *you can*, as in *one can* (impersonal pronoun). But he was born and bred in Brooklyn. He doesn't use the word *one* for the general third person pronoun. He says what almost everyone does, you. As in:

> You can lead a horse to water, but you can't make him drink.

20

Compare that with:

> One can lead a horse to a water trough, but one cannot make him or her sip of the water thereof.

The second, while much more erudite and specific, would never be heard outside of a Shakespeare play. Maybe, and if you don't viscerally and prejudicially hate the man, you can lend him the benefit of the doubt. He was saying something to the effect of, "Can you believe these women? What they'll allow a star or famous person to do? It's nuts!"

Would Mr. Trump do such a thing? I don't know him, but from words I've heard him say in public, I'd have to say if a woman were to allow him to place his hand on her crotch he may very well take the opportunity. Did he? He has said he takes the opportunity, not always invited, to at least attempt to steal a kiss from women he's attracted to. Boorish behavior? Yes. Something more acceptable in days gone by? Certainly. Has he been violent with women? I don't think so, but there are still unresolved law suits against him. Call me old-fashioned, but I still go with the innocent-until-proven-guilty theory.

But, to be fair to the anti-trumpers, what of his record of "unwanted sexual contacts?" In May 2016 *The New York Times* (by the way, noted for being solidly in the Clinton camp and even more solidly anti-Trump during the entire presidential campaign and now continuing into his presidency) published an article titled *Crossing the Line: How Donald Trump Behaved with Women in Private*, by

Michael Barbaro and Megan Twohey. The following information comes from a Wikipedia article.[7]

Herewith, a summary.

Fifty women were interviewed for the story. Many of those who had worked for Mr. Trump or had other business dealings with him reported that "they had never known Mr. Trump to objectify women or treat them with disrespect." Mr. Trump was said to be supportive of their professional ambitions as well as necessities of motherhood. Many of those interviewed stated they had never received any unwanted attention or made to feel at all uncomfortable in any way. As quoted in the Wikipedia article, "Laura Kirilova Chukanov, a Bulgarian immigrant and 2009 Miss USA pageant contestant, said that Trump helped her make connections for a documentary that she was working on about her home country."

There are those who disagree, of course.

Jessica Leeds accused Mr. Trump of assaulting her as she sat next to him in a first class cabin on a flight returning to New York from the Midwest. She said he put his hand on her breasts and tried to put a hand up her skirt. She said he "was like an octopus." A spokesman for Mr. Trump, Jason Miller, responded to the allegations, saying they were "fiction." These charges only became known in the final months of the campaign and are considered by the Trump team as politically motivated. An alleged witness to the case, Antony Gilberthorpe, a county councilor from Gloucestershire, England claims he saw nothing of the sort

---

7

https://en.wikipedia.org/wiki/Donald_Trump_sexual_misconduct_all egations happen. *The Times* made note of questions concerning Mr. Gilberthorpe's veracity.

Kristen Anderson, as reported in *The Washington Post* on October 14, 2016, claims that Mr. Trump groped her in a Manhattan night club in the early 1990s. She says she decided to come forward after other women led the way.

Cathy Heller, reported by *The Guardian* (a British newspaper), claims some two decades earlier that Mr. Trump "grabbed and kissed her" at his Mar-a-Lago country club, where her parents were members. The account was corroborated by family members who were present. The incident allegedly occurred in 1997, but Ms. Heller decided to come forward only after Mr. Trump had declared his candidacy for the presidency. Ms. Heller was a supporter of Mr. Trump's main challenger, Hillary Clinton. Trump spokesmen deny Ms. Heller's accusation, saying it is politically motivated.

Temple McDowell accused Mr. Trump of "unwanted kisses and embraces," according to a report in *The New York Times* in May 2016. The incident in question allegedly occurred in 1997 during the Miss USA contest. Ms. McDowell, previously Temple Taggart, was Miss Utah at the time. Mr. Trump has denied the claim. Ms. McDowell has stated that she is a Republican and not a supporter of Hillary Clinton.

Karena Virginia claimed at a press conference for Gloria Allred in October 2016 that she met Mr. Trump waiting for a ride at the U.S. Open in Queens, NY. She claimed he approached her in a group of other men, made a comment about her legs, and "grabbed her right arm, then his hand touched my breast." Jessica Ditto, Trump campaign spokeswoman, replied with a statement including, "Discredited political operative Gloria Allred, in another coordinated, publicity seeking attack with the Clinton campaign, will stop at nothing to smear Mr. Trump."

Mindy McGillivray, in an article in the *Palm Beach Post*, claims that in 2003 in a crowd at Mr. Trump's Mar-a-Lago estate she "felt a grab, a little nudge." She said at first she thought it was from a friend's camera bag, but when she turned around she saw Mr. Trump suddenly look away. She told her friend, Ken Davidoff, "Donald just grabbed my ass!" The incident was never reported to authorities. She says she only came forward when she heard Mr. Trump deny this type of behavior during a presidential debate. Trump's press secretary has denied the claim, a denial backed up by Darryl Davidoff, the brother of Ken Davidoff. According to Darryl, "I do not believe it really happened. Nobody saw it happen and she just wanted to be in the limelight."

Rachel Crooks, a receptionist in an office in Trump Tower Manhattan, accused Mr. Trump of overly aggressive behavior when she was in an elevator with him. She says she shook hands with Trump, but he would not release her hand. According to Crooks, Trump "began kissing her cheeks, then directly on the mouth." Mr. Trump disputes the claim.

Natasha Stoynoff was a "journalist" for *People Magazine*. She interviewed Mr. Trump and Melania Trump at his Mar-a-Lago estate in 2005. She asserts that during a tour of the estate Mr. Trump forced her against a wall and kissed her. Mr. Trump has said publicly that the event never occurred, pointing out that Ms. Stoynoff wrote nothing about the allegation in her *People Magazine* article. Ms. Stoynoff's response was that she only publicized the event after she was angered by Mr. Trumps claim during a presidential debate that he has never assaulted a woman and because of the *Access Hollywood* "pussy" statement release in October, 2016. Ms. Stoynoff said Mr. Trump only stopped trying to kiss her when his butler, Anthony Senecal, "burst into the room." Mr. Senecal has stated for the record that he would never "burst" into a room, but would knock and wait for permission to enter. He said he did enter the room in question, but saw nothing that would cause him to believe anything untoward had occurred. Further, the alleged incident took place in a room with windows on all sides, making it a very unlikely place for anyone to attempt such a thing.

Jessica Drake accused Mr. Trump of assaulting her and two acquaintances in 2006. The accusation became public during the previously mentioned news conference called by her lawyer, Gloria Allred. (That name keeps coming up. Coincidence?) Drake said Trump met her at a golf tournament in Lake Tahoe and was invited to meet with him in his hotel suite. Feeling uncomfortable going alone, she invited two friends to accompany her. Drake says that Trump "grabbed [hugged] each of us tightly... and kissed each one without asking permission." Drake also claims Trump later offered her $10,000 to join him in his suite and offered to take her back to Los Angeles in his private jet. A Trump campaign spokesman said the allegations are "false and ridiculous." In response to a photo of Mr. Trump with Ms. Drake at the tournament, the spokesman stated "[t]he picture is one of thousands taken out of respect for people asking to have their picture taken with Mr. Trump." According to the Trump campaign, the story was "just another attempt by the Clinton campaign to defame [Mr. Trump]."

Ninni Laaksonen was Miss Finland in 2006 and appeared with Mr. Trump on the David Letterman show in that year. She claims that before they went on the air Mr. Trump grabbed her buttocks. She said she doesn't believe anyone saw it. The report was not public made until Ms. Laaksonen was interviewed by a Finnish Newspaper in October, 2016.

Summer Zervos was a contestant in an episode of "The Apprentice" television show in 2005. She is now represented by Gloria Allred. (There's that name again. Might it be a franchise?) Zervos alleges that when she approached Trump in 2007 about a job she was invited to meet him at the Beverly Hills Hotel. She claims Trump kissed her, groped her breasts, and thrust his genitals toward her, all non-consensually. John Barry, cousin to Zervos, has stated that she was a supporter of the Trump candidacy and told others how he had helped her out. Zervos invited Mr. Trump to dine at a restaurant but he declined the invitation. Summer Zervos also sent an email to the Trump campaign, after the alleged event, expressing her desire to reconnect with Trump. (I'll let the reader determine whether Ms. Zervos' behavior seems in the least consistent.)

Cassandra Searles was Miss Washington in the Miss USA pageant in 2013. *Rolling Stone* and NPR (there's an unbiased news service) reported that she was fondled by Mr. Trump at the pageant. *Yahoo!News* also ran an article concerning a Facebook posting by Ms. Searles in which she stated Mr. Trump made unwanted advances to her. She accused him of groping her buttocks and inviting her to his hotel room. There has been no response to Searles' allegations from the Trump campaign or his current administration.

There have also been allegations of Mr. Trump entering beauty contest dressing rooms. Trump owned the Miss Universe franchise from 1996 to 2015, and stated on the Howard Stern Show that he did, in fact, enter the dressing rooms unannounced. "[T]hey're standing there with no clothes. And you see these incredible-looking women. And so I sort of get away with things like that ... I'll go backstage before a show, and everyone's getting dressed and ready and everything else." There have been accusations of Mr. Trump entering the dressing rooms, but at the 1997 Miss Teen USA Pageant, where Mariah Billardo says Trump entered the dressing room, eleven other women who were in the room at the time stated they did not see him. They also said the room was large and they may have been somewhere else at the time. He admitted to a national radio audience to entering dressing rooms but obviously did nothing to draw attention to himself. Rude? Yes. Get over it. Most of the former contestants interviewed "were doubtful of or dismissed the possibility that Trump violated their changing room privacy." Former Miss Massachusetts (Teen USA) Jessica Granata said, with respect to allegations of Trump's "dressing room escapades," There were so many chaperones, I can't even fathom ... It was very secure."

Bridget Sullivan, Miss New Hampshire USA 2000, in an interview with *BuzzFeed*, said Mr. Trump entered the women's dressing room to wish them good luck. Other women who were in the room remember nothing of the alleged incident and other contestants reported that they had no negative interactions with him. A Trump spokesman has said Ms. Sullivan's claims are false.

Tasha Dixon, Miss Arizona USA in 2001, told a reporter from the local CBS affiliate station that during the pageant Mr. Trump entered the women's dressing room unannounced. Trump spokesman, Jessica Ditto, stated the "accusations have no merit and have already been disproven by many other individuals who were present."

She also said she believes the accusation was politically motivated.

Samantha Carol Holvey, Miss North Carolina USA 2006, has stated that Mr. Trump's behavior around the women in the pageant was "creepy," but says he made no improper advances toward her.

Whew! That's quite a list. But what Trump's detractors seem to be missing, better stated, *ignoring*, is not that he is aggressive toward beautiful women, but that this is so common as to be a non-story. Politics is the exercise of power. Who, besides those who strongly desire to exercise power over others would jump into the political cesspool? Politics is, at its core, all about making people do things they don't want to do, or keeping them from doing things they do want to do. Else, why would we have to enforce political decisions, laws and regulations, with people in government-issued uniforms carrying guns? Sexual abuse is rampant among the political class and their hangers on. This is not an excuse, it's just a fact of real life. Just look at the headlines:

Sir Edward Heath WAS a pedophile, says police chief. Astonishing claim is made that the former PM is guilty of vile crimes 'covered up by the Establishment.[8]

DHS Insider: Pedogate Exposes CIA-Mossad Deep State. CIA-Mossad hate Putin for saving Syria, their stepping stone to Iranian oil.[9]

---

8 http://www.thetruthseeker.co.uk/?cat=93
9 https://www.henrymakow.com/2017/02/Pedogate-Exposes-CIA-Mossad-Deep-State.html

The Child Porn Pentagon-NSA-CIA Link 'They' Don't Want You to Know. Two senior U.S. intelligence officials admitted that an "unbelievable" amount of child pornography has been found on the NSA work computers.[10]

Fmr House Speaker Says Child He Raped Should Pay Back Hush Money Since He Broke His Silence. Illustrating how pedophilia is endemic among the political class, Hastert also happens to be good friends with the Podestas.[11]

Power, Pedophilia and the US Government. As the West charges full speed ahead towards World War III with its incendiary epicenter Ukraine, simultaneous headlines are breaking with pedophilia sex scandals implicating the highest levels of elite power and privilege involving both US presidents and the British royal family.[12]

Time Magazine online[13] (undated) ran a story titled **"Top 10 Political Sex Scandals,"** listing Mark Sanford, John Ensign, David Vitter, Kwame Kilpatrick, Larry Craig, Barney Frank, Bill Clinton, Eliot Spitzer, John Edwards, and Anthony Weiner as only the **"top ten."**

---

10 https://www.rallypoint.com/shared-links/the-child-porn-pentagon-nsa-cia-link-they-don-t-want-you-to-know
11 http://thefreethoughtproject.com/hastert-hush-money-child-rapist/
12 http://www.veteranstoday.com/2015/02/07/power-pedophilia-and-the-us-government/
13 http://content.time.com/time/specials/2007/article/0,28804,1721111_1721210_1906894,00.html

The editors must have had a difficult time paring the list down to such a small number. And these are only American government scandals. How about we take a trip back in time and across the pond...

> **1963: The Profumo Scandal.**[14] At the height of the cold war in the early 60s, as the established order was challenged as never before, Britons paid rapt attention to a sordid little affair which involved a cabinet minister, a showgirl and a Soviet naval attaché.

> *The Telegraph,* a British newspaper, in their online edition of February 22, 2017, ran a story, *A brief history of political scandals* [15] , Jeffrey Archer (Tory MP), accused of having sex with a prostitute.

And it's not just a problem with the politically powerful...

> **Elijah Wood: Hollywood Is Run By A Powerful Elite Pedophile Ring.** The star of Lord of the Rings warns the entertainment industry is infested with vipers ready to prey on the vulnerable.[16]

> **The Televangelists' Hall of Shame** [17] lists the sexual dalliances of "Christian"

---

14 https://www.britannica.com/event/Profumo-affair
https://www.theguardian.com/politics/2001/apr/10/past.derekbrown
15 http://www.telegraph.co.uk/news/politics/7503870/A-brief-history-of-political-scandals.html
16 https://www.davidicke.com/article/402814/elijah-wood-hollywood-run-powerful-elite-paedophile-ring
17 http://home.earthlink.net/~19ranger57/halosham.htm

luminaries Jim Bakker, Jimmy Swaggart, and Pat Robertson.

I could go on and on and on with other examples from every government and corporation in the world. Volumes have been written on the subject. Let's not forget Eisenhower had at least one mistress that we know about, that Jack and Bobby Kennedy were notorious for their extramarital activities, their brother Edward was famous for Chappaquiddick and causing the death of Mary Jo Kopechne, and their father's and grandfather's amorous adventures with women who were not their wives were well known if not acknowledged in that gentler time. Johnson was possibly the crudest man to ever inhabit The White House and hardly met a woman he didn't try to bed, some successfully if that can be believed,[18] and Bill Clinton was certainly accused of more sexual indiscretion and even sexual *violence* than any person who has ever occupied that office.

Power, it is said, is an aphrodisiac. This has been true from the earliest recorded history of mankind. I'll leave the explanation of why that may be the case to the experts. But the theory that the same psychological drivers that push humans to the top of organizations in which they have power over others, possibly the same brain chemistry, is also responsible for a heightened sex drive makes sense, at least to this author. One can easily imagine any of these people saying, in the vein of Madelyn Albright, "What's the use of having all this power if you don't abuse it once in a while?"[19] There's a certain socio-pathology inherent in all

---

18 Caro, Robert, The Path To Power (The Years of Lyndon Johnson), Vintage (February 17, 1990)
19 "What's the point of having this superb military that you're always talking about if we can't use it?" Madeleine Albright to Colin Powell,

political leaders. A profession that is based in half-truths and manipulation of information for the benefit of chosen groups within society can only attract those who are of the "end justifies the means" persuasion and not opposed to a little larceny, or more. Idealists, honest persons, and those with a moral compass need not apply. Those who do get swept up in the political maelstrom with an initial idealistic drive quickly leave the environment or change their manner of thinking and behaving in order to survive. Those who are best at lying, deceiving, and manipulating people and information for their own benefit and aggrandizement will rise to the top. In our world, the top of the top, the *Capo de Tutti Capi* is the president of the United States.

None of this is to excuse any aggressive behavior by Donald Trump, but only to make the point that making a point of it, as if this behavior is somehow unusual and should disqualify him from office, is petty and ridiculous. If all candidates and office holders accused of or found to be guilty of aggressive or even predatory sexual behavior were disqualified from office we'd have no government. There are those who believe that would be an improvement, but again, that's a subject for another book.

---

as quoted in Madam Secretary, A Memoir (2003), p. 182, by Madeleine Albright.

Mr. Trump's detractors say he could have put his inheritance in the stock market and done just as well. Could this be true? Let's look at the facts.

It seems no one really knows exactly how much Donald Trump actually inherited from his father, Fred. Donald mentioned the figure of a million dollars. Mark Rubio claimed it was one-hundred million. Searching the internet, both seem to be highly inaccurate. The most likely number seems to be in the neighborhood of $40,000,000. This wasn't cash, but equity in various real estate properties and other investments. Donald Trump was also the beneficiary of a loan from his father, in addition to loan guarantees, and the incalculable value in the New York real estate development market of the family name.

According to Matt Palumbo,[20] If Donald Trump could have liquidated the estimated $40,000,000 inheritance, which in itself is doubtful, and invested that cash in a stock market equity account that returned the equivalent of the increase in the Standard and Poor 500 Index, and had spent *none* of it since the date of his father's death, he would still not have anywhere near the net worth that he claims today. Basing the value only on the S&P 500 Index gross increase over that time completely ignores taxes and management fees; dividends are taxable income, even if they are reinvested. Mr. Palumbo estimates that Donald Trump, if he could have invested the entire forty million in an S&P 500 fund, would today have, after all expenses and taxes, $1.91 billion, far shy of the $3.7 billion he claims.

---

20 http://streetcarnage.com/blog/trumps-inheritance-would-not-have-made-more-money-in-the-stock-market/

That is considered an accurate figure, even by his detractors.

Those who claim Mr. Trump doesn't have the business talent he claims also ignore the most common path of family businesses and wealth, a path that is so common it is almost a cliché: The first generation creates the wealth, the second generation sustains it, and the third generation loses it. Let's also not ignore the habit of lottery winners to end up broke and in debt. Donald has certainly done better than sustain his father's business.

Yes, but... Some companies in which Mr. Trump has been principal shareholder have declared bankruptcy. The point being???

People who make this statement demonstrate their ignorance of business. We can expect this, as most Americans have been educated in a government school system that increasingly disingenuously teaches business is inherently predatory, unscrupulous, and detrimental to the interests of the common man. According to government-approved text bookss, were it not for government, greedy, capitalistic businessmen would destroy not only individuals but the very fabric of American society itself.

In fact, starting a business is incredibly risky and difficult. Twelve startups fail in the first two years for every successful venture. Far from indicating Mr. Trump is not the business genius he claims to be, the fact that some of his ventures, even with all his money and experience, do not succeed should provide evidence of just how difficult starting and running a business actually is, and should give people some appreciation for the risk that entrepreneurs take to start businesses that pay wages and salaries to hundreds of millions of Americans and provide the taxes that sustain the government.

The fact is, in the rough and tumble world of real estate development, Donald Trump is a Yuuuuuuge! success.

Bigot: a person who is obstinately or intolerantly devoted to his or her own opinions and prejudices; especially: one who regards or treats the members of a group (as a racial or ethnic group) with hatred and intolerance. (Merriam-Webster Online Dictionary)

Is Donald Trump obstinately or intolerantly devoted to his own opinions and prejudices? From any objective view, it would seem he's fairly fluid in his opinions and willing to adapt to those that result in the greatest profit or benefit to him and his businesses. He's changed political parties five times, so he's obviously willing to publicly admit that he can change his mind and way of thinking. He was a supporter of Ronald Reagan in the 80s, switched to the Reform Party in 1999, then from 2001 to 2008 identified himself as a Democrat. He registered as an Independent in late 2011, then changed to Republican again late in 2012. He may be described as an opportunist but *obstinately and intolerantly devoted to his own opinions* does not seem an apt description of the man. That he is *not* obstinately wedded to his beliefs may be a valid criticism, but that he is a bigot seems to be an irrational conclusion, if the word has any meaning.

As stated above, whether he agrees or disagrees with the U.S. Supreme Court decisions on abortion and gay marriage, he has stated publicly that these are decisions that have been made, and as Chief Executive he will enforce applicable law. In an interview with Leslie Stahl, when she asked him to elaborate on his views on same-sex marriage, Mr. Trump said, "It's irrelevant because it was already settled. It's law. It was settled in the Supreme Court." Where is his obstinacy in that, unless he's obstinately saying he'll follow the law and do the job as president as specified in the Constitution? Social Justice Warriors want him to lie prostrate and claim the superiority of the Revolution, *a la* Chairman Mao's China. Is it not enough that he states the law of the land and states that he'll do his duty as president to follow it? No, they want full obeisance to the cognoscenti and proclaim his absolute agreement with them. Not only must he don sack cloth and ashes and tear out his beard, but he must publicly and loudly apologize for his past sins of incorrect thinking and beg forgiveness of the public he has so offended.

What about those violent thugs that seemed to magically appear up at his political rallies and campaign stops? (I'm not saying which faction or person actually organized or funded the violence, but his initials are George Soros.) At no time did Mr. Trump even intimate he supported violence against anyone, but was still questioned about this. He replied in a televised interview on the program *60 Minutes*, "I am so saddened to hear that. And I say, 'Stop it.' If it — if it helps, I will say this, and I will say right to the cameras: Stop it." Murder, mayhem, and violence are hallmarks of the Clinton regime, not Trump Enterprises. I know of no accusations of Mr. Trump having silenced his opponents with anything other than tough negotiating and money, the stuff of capitalism and business.

Is Mr. Trump a Mexican hater? This criticism seems to stem from his desire to enforce the laws of the United States against illegal immigration and criticism of a California judge, Gonzalo Curiel. Mr. Trump has stated for the record his objection to Judge Curiel presiding over a case in which one of Mr. Trump's businesses is the defendant. This has absolutely nothing to do with the fact that Curiel is of Mexican descent. It has everything to do, however, with his membership in *La Raza* (Spanish for

"The Race") *Lawyers Association of California.* The organization's stated purpose and goals: The purpose and goal of this Association is to promote the interests of the Latino communities throughout the state and the professional interests of the membership. The organization also supports pro-immigrant alien organizations, regardless of whether an individual is in the United States legally or illegally. As it is one of Mr. Trump's stated goals to enforce immigration laws, those who have publicly condoned illegal immigration and have stated they will defend illegal immigrants can only be seen as biased. A citizen involved in legal proceedings is allowed to contest judge and jury when it is apparent that they are biased against him.

That many of the illegal immigrants from south of the U.S. border are not desirable as citizens of this country is not debatable. But stating that fact is one of the many, many third rails of American politics. Mr. Trump touched that rail, and will forever be thought of as a bigot, a racist, and as prejudiced against Mexicans. Of course, those who are prejudiced against conservative values, which include a sane and orderly management of immigration, can scream anything they want against Mr. Trump and never be called to defend themselves. Trump's words were, "When Mexico sends its people, they're not sending their best... They're bringing drugs, their crime, their rapists." (And then he continued, "And some, I assume, are good people." This last statement is all but ignored.) Mr. Trump's opponents contend that he said "They're rapists." But no objective, honest hearing or reading of that speech could interpret Mr. Trump's "their" for "they're." In English, they're, their, and there are pronounced exactly the same. But taken in context, his clear meaning was "their." There is no other honest interpretation of the word. Mr. Trump employs hundreds if not thousands of people of Mexican descent, of legal Mexican immigrants. Can anyone honestly believe he would do so if he believed all Mexicans to be rapists?

With that said, it is a sad fact that rape is epidemic among illegal immigrants from south of the border. Women are told this before they undertake the journey. It's expected, as if rape were simply part of the cost of the journey. And what recourse do they have? Can an illegal immigrant report her rapist to the police? (Can an illegal immigrant report *his* rapist to the police? Surely you don't believe this is a problem only women and girls experience.) The issue cannot be approached from any rational standpoint. Even though Mr. Trump employs thousands of Blacks and Latinos and enjoys their support, the charge of racism and bigotry will never go away. The Social Justice Warriors will see to that.

Is Donald Trump anti-Jewish? There are certainly no limitations on any race or ethnicity joining one of his golf clubs or staying at one of his hotels or resorts. Up until at least August 18, 2016, all of Donald Trump's adult children were either married to or dating Jews.[21] Ivanka converted to the Jewish religion. Donald Jr. is married to Vanessa Haydon, Jewish. Eric Trump is married to Lara Yunaska, Jewish. They were married at Mar-a-Lago, a club that did not allow Jews to be members until Donald Trump sued them over the policy (before he owned the enterprise). Many executives in Mr. Trump's organization are Jewish. Leaders in Mr. Trump's presidential campaign were Jews. There is no evidence, absolutely none, that Mr. Trump is anti-Semitic.

---

21 Statement made by Ezra Lavant at
https://www.youtube.com/watch?v=U2G9MR1n7Es&feature=youtube

His policies? Trump stated in a campaign speech, "I refuse to allow America to become a place where gay people, Christian people, Jewish people are targets of persecution and intimidation by radical Islamic preachers of hate and violence." He tweeted five years ago, *"The White House should stop publicly pressuring Israel on Iran. Iran's nuclear program is the threat, not Israel's right to self-defense."* Another tweet from 2012, *"Bad move-@BarackObama released $174M in aid to the Palestinians... That money is going to Hamas."* According to Ezra Levant, there has never been a more pro-Israel candidate.

Referring to Donald trump as a bigot is nothing more than a smoke screen and appeal to pure emotion by and for people who do not have the intelligence to identify and debate real issues.

Good heavens! Can we not finally put this ridiculous assertion to rest? Mr. Trump is sometimes physically demonstrative during a speech, but the physical gyrations during this particular speech were imitative of a flustered person in general. If one were to observe every speech Mr. Trump made on the campaign trail, one would observe the same more than once, and not in reference to the reporter in question. If one were to review Ms. Clinton's speeches, one would see the same. Intelligent adults simply don't make fun of handicapped people. His critics question his intelligence, but that only sheds light on their lack of same. Mr. Trump has stated emphatically that he was not imitating a physical disability and didn't even remember the reporter in question had a disability. If nothing else, Donald Trump fesses up to his crimes. He is brutally honest about what he feels and thinks, one of the qualities so many millions of voters appreciated and helped elect him to office.

No more needs be said about this. It's a non-issue.

Has Mr. Trump ever stated that Muslims are terrorists? Are dangerous? Easy answer: no. Has he said *some* Muslims are terrorists? Has he said *some* are dangerous? I'm not sure if he's ever used those specific words, but he has certainly made statements that would lead any rational person to the conclusion that he does, in fact, believe that to be true. And why not?

Leaving aside the causes of the hatred towards western governments and people by Islamist extremists, no one of any level of intelligence above that of a box of hair can argue that there is not a disproportionate representation in the world of terrorism by those of the Muslim faith.

Do Christians commit atrocities? Yes, and if there were a significant proportion of Christian terrorist immigrants, it would be the duty of the chief executive of the branch of government charged with enforcing the laws of the land to enforce current laws or write new laws that would serve to protect the safety of the American people from Christian terrorists. However, with that said, there is, in fact, no noticeable problem with Christian terrorist immigrants.

Do Hindus commit atrocities? Yes, and if there were a high proportion of Hindu terrorist immigrants, it would be the duty of the chief executive of the branch of government charged with enforcing the laws of the land to enforce current laws or write new laws that would serve to protect the safety of the American people from Hindu terrorists. However, with that said, there is, in fact, no noticeable problem with Hindu terrorist immigrants.

Do Jews commit atrocities? Yes, and if there were a high proportion of Jewish terrorists immigrants, it would be the duty of the chief executive of the branch of government charged with enforcing the laws of the land to enforce current laws or write new laws that would serve to protect the safety of the American people from Jewish terrorists. However, with that said, there is in fact no noticeable problem with Jewish terrorist immigrants.

Enough. You get the point. There have been dozens of people arrested and convicted in the United States for terrorism-related crimes since 9/11 who were born in the seven countries Mr. Trump listed in an executive order, the purpose of which was to delay immigration specifically targeted at countries defined by the preceding (Obama) administration. If Mr. Trump erred, it was in not including more regions among those whose immigrants should receive extra scrutiny. His detractors will point out that the statistical chance of being killed by a terrorist in the U.S. is so miniscule as to be irrelevant. Point taken. But the chance of being murdered by a *non-terrorist* is also miniscule for most people. The author of this small volume, for example, is still alive after sixty years, but still the government goes to great lengths to prevent murder and prosecute those responsible for it when they are caught.

Katie Hopkins published an article in the *Daily Mail* about the problems experienced by women in Sweden with immigrants from primarily Muslim countries.[22] She writes,

> *One lady* [in a women's multi-faith center] *explained: there is a strange moral code here in Rinkeby* [Sweden]. *You are much more exposed to crime* [committed by Muslim men] *if you are not a*

22 http://www.dailymail.co.uk/news/article-4269576/KATIE-HOPKINS-reports-Scandi-lib-paradise-Sweden.html

Muslim. These boys think they can take everything from a woman who is not wearing a hijab or at least covers her hair.

Another... told me: we don't go out on the streets here after dark. It is too dangerous. I have lived here for 25 years and it has gotten worse and worse. The situation now is so tense that it is impossible for me to go to, say, the supermarket to get some milk.

This video explains what has happened in Sweden and is happening in other European countries. Mr. Trump, his supporters, and in fact every rational person wants to avoid in the United States what is happening in Sweden and other European countries that have opened their borders to millions of Muslim immigrants. The person who posted the video says, "This video I found explains what mass Muslim migration has done to Sweden and the bleak future Sweden has over the next few decades. The Swedish far left liberal approach has destroyed their own country. Sweden is no longer the image you once had...

Swedenstan has arrived.
https://www.youtube.com/watch?v=vZ-nwoijTpQ&t=4s

The same is happening in Germany, France, Britain and other countries that have allowed unchecked mass immigration from Muslim states.

The *Daily Mail*[23] reports that women in the district of Chapelle-Pajol in eastern Paris claim they cannot leave their houses without being verbally abused by migrant men. The area is said to have become more and more dangerous for women over the past year as young African

---

23 http://www.dailymail.co.uk/news/article-4529372/The-no-zone-women-PARIS.html

and Arab men flood the area. Over 18,000 people have signed a petition urging Paris authorities to highlight the harassment, drug-dealing and crime plaguing the area.

Mr. Trump has said he'd like to "shut down Muslims entering the United States until our country's representatives can figure out what is going on." This was during a time of unprecedented attacks on Germany, France, Great Britain, and Canada. Almost as certain as the sun rising tomorrow morning, when we look into these Muslim terrorists, we invariably find they spent time in a Muslim country being further radicalized and trained to better attack us. There are millions upon millions of young Muslim men who would welcome death as they kill as many *infidels* as possible, and an infidel is anyone—man, woman, child, old, young—who is not Muslim. There are a hundred million people, give or take, in the United States who would prefer that we not allow these people in or back in as the case may be. More, it is entirely within the rights of Americans to make that demand and for the president to enforce it through existing law.

Let us not single out Mr. Trump. It is a fact that President Obama, during his two terms in office was often referred to by immigration groups as the *Deporter in Chief*. During his administration, up until and through the year 2015, Immigration Services and other legal bodies deported more than two and a half million people. This does not include those who left voluntarily before enduring legal proceedings or were caught and turned away at the border. The government's own data shows that Mr. Obama deported more people than any other prior administration and, in fact, deported more than all other administrations during the twentieth century.

Of course, the mainstream Hillary-supporting media has a short and very selective memory. They use Mr. Trump's statement that he will faithfully execute the duties of his office and enforce the laws of the land with respect to immigration as a foundation and build upon it a wall of half-truths and innuendos until the concept has somehow morphed into a vision among the populace of a Trump-America where Muslims are randomly picked up off the street and thrown in a van, never to be seen again.

But this isn't just a "terrorist" problem. It's a *clash of cultures*. When a million men (actually more) who believe that any show of flesh by a woman is an invitation to rape enter a society where women dress in western-style clothing, there are going to be severe and pronounced problems. Due to the *Religion of Diversity* in these United States, immigrants are no longer expected to adapt themselves to their new surroundings, to assimilate. For some unknowable reason, liberal society and the *Religion of Diversity* demands that the native population bend its morals and adapt its customs to suit the newcomers. Some people might see this as part of a grand plan to meld all cultures into one, or to dissolve the notion of culture altogether, in preparation for a One-World Government. George Soros, if he were to ever be as honest about his beliefs and goals as Donald Trump, would certainly agree.

Mr. Trump has never stated he wants to deport Muslims. He has said he wants to deport *illegal immigrants*. Enforcing the law is, in fact, exactly his job as president as defined in the Constitution. He has never suggested a ban on all Muslim immigrants. He stated he wants to put a temporary hold on immigration from known terrorist-producing countries until such time as we have better techniques of vetting immigrant applicants. This is purely within the purview of his responsibility as president and a completely rational recommendation, given the violence and mayhem any rational person may observe going on around the world perpetrated by a disproportionate number of young, Muslim men.

Referring to the facts, something most Trump-haters are loath to do, a 1952 federal statute permits the president to suspend the immigration status of any person or group whose entry into the United States might impair public health or safety or national security. Mr. Obama and other presidents have used the same law to do exactly what Mr. Trump has proposed.

Yet again, a rational review of the facts does not show that Mr. Trump wants to impose a Muslim ban or deport Muslims. The government's primary job is to protect the life, liberty, and property of its citizens. It seems to me that is Donald Trump's goal.

"The bill before us will certainly do some good," he said, standing before the country on the Senate floor. He praised the legislation, saying it would provide "better fences and better security along our borders" and would "help stem some of the tide of illegal immigration in this country."

Senator Obama *was talking about the* Secure Fence Act of 2006, *legislation authorizing a physical barrier along the southern border* [passed into law with the signature of President George W. Bush and] *with the support of 26 Democratic senators including Obama and party leaders such as Hillary Clinton, Joe Biden, and Chuck Schumer.*[24]

The Secure Fence Act referenced above authorized the building of a 700-mile long double-layer fence on the border between Mexico and the United States. When it was begun it had the support of the Mexican government. We were concerned with illegal immigration; Mexico was concerned with the influx of guns the drug cartels were using to fight a war of attrition against Mexican law enforcement. Hillary Clinton denied supporting a wall between the U.S. and Mexico, making a distinction between "fence" and "wall," reminiscent of her husband's quibbling over the definition of "is" during some embarrassing impeachment hearings. The fact is, the last president, Hillary Clinton, Donald Trump, and a majority of congress-critters (of the class of 2006) agree that a wall

---

24 https://www.bostonglobe.com/news/politics/2017/01/26/when-wall-was-fence-and-democrats-embraced/QE7ieCBXjXVxO63pLMTe9O/story.html

along the border would help to control illegal immigration. Trump says wall. Hillary says fence. Tomato, tom*ah*to.

Mr. Trump's detractors in government, as all politicians, have a short memory because they know the American people's collective memory is even shorter. They are fully aware that the presstitute[25] mainstream media will print whatever they are given and the Booboisie of America will believe what they are told. Mr. Trump wants to build a fence along the Mexican border? Why, he's a racist! Obama and Clinton and a majority of congress authorized funding for the same thing? Ignore that man behind the curtain! The Great Oz has spoken!

They're also up in arms that Mr. Trump expects Mexico to pay for the wall. In Mr. Trump's view, Mexico's government policies are the cause of that country's economic difficulties; it is the economic environment they themselves have created that force millions of Mexicans to seek a better life in the United States. Therefore, they should shoulder some, if not all, of the cost of constraining the illegal flow of their citizens across U.S. borders. Looking at the question from a purely business standpoint, it's estimated that the U.S. has a trade imbalance of $58 billion with Mexico—we buy $58 billion more of goods produced in Mexico than they buy produced by U.S industry. Certainly the U.S. government could rightfully impose trade restrictions, duties, and taxes to reverse that imbalance. Ignoring the economic theories and realities giving the lie to the idea that that would help the U.S. economy in any way, still, Mr. Trump can easily make the case that spending $10 billion on a wall for the purposes of maintaining their trading status under NAFTA, or to avoid

---

25 I am thankful to Paul Craig Roberts for coining this term.
https://lewrockwell.com/author/paul-craig-roberts/

punitive duties and imposts would be in Mexico's best interests.

And let us not forget, Donald Trump is first and foremost a businessman. In any deal, getting someone else to pay the freight just makes good sense. Why should we be surprised that he enters negotiations with that demand?

In any rational world the immigration issue would be a matter of calm, reasoned discussion. Documented history of both sides shows that the federal government wants to control immigration and deport people who are here illegally. That this issue has become evidence of another brick in Mr. Trump's "Nazi" wall is nothing more than evidence of the Clinton-supporting mainstream media's, and their extremely well-financed liberal ownership's, influence over the U.S. populace. Were democrats in power, the mainstream media would be proclaiming the benefits of a wall (fence) along the border. With Republicans holding the White House and both houses of Congress, the MSM are foursquare against it. And because the mainstream media virtually controls the opinion of the Booboisie here in the Land of the Free and Home of the Brave (sic), they were able to stir up a storm of indignation against the issue.

This is nothing more than a tempest in a teapot to steer the attention of the ultra-sensitive American public away from the real issues, the complicated, nuanced issues the MSM under control of the Deep State would rather not publicize.

SCREED NUMBER EIGHT: DONALD TRUMP IS CRUDE, A LOOSE CANNON

When Harry Truman's daughter was publically criticized by a music critic of the *Washington Post* for her creative efforts, the president responded to the critic: "Someday I hope to meet you. When that happens you'll need a new nose, a lot of beefsteak for black eyes, and perhaps a supporter below."

On another occasion, a journalist referred to the president as "a thin-lipped hater." The president replied that the journalist was "a rat" and a "guttersnipe."

But we still admire "Give-'em-hell Harry" and count him in the top tier of American presidents.

Theodore Roosevelt is famous for living on the thin line between sanity and insanity. Certainly Lyndon Johnson holds the record for crudeness in thought and word. When asked by a reporter in a private Oval Office meeting why the United States military was in Vietnam, President Johnson stood, unzipped his pants, extracted the symbol of his manhood, and wagged the presidential member in the reporters face. "This is why," he said.[26]

His critics point to the executive order, 13769, stopping immigration from seven named countries where immigrant backgrounds are difficult or impossible to ascertain. For example, in Syria there is no U.S. embassy or Consulate, making it only reasonable to stop immigration from that country until an effective vetting process can be implemented. Critics specifically use the confusion and travel delays caused by the executive order

---

26 Robert Dallek, Flawed Giant: Lyndon Johnson and His Times, 1961-1975 (NY: Oxford University Press, 1998) p. 491.

as proof of Mr. Trump's deficiencies in effectively operating under government procedures. However, the executive order in question gave authority to The State Department and Department of Homeland Security to handle individual cases *at their discretion*. Specifically, said Mr. Trump, "I permitted the Secretary of State and the Secretary of Homeland Security to jointly grant case-by-case waivers when they determined that it was in the national interest to do so."

Was this executive order intended to discriminate against Muslims? Paragraph 1-b-iv states that the order does not "provide a basis for discriminating for or against members *of any particular religion*." While the order allows for the prioritization of refugee claims from members of persecuted religious minority groups, that priority is to be applied to refugees from every nation mentioned in the executive order, including those in which Islam is a minority religion.

It is no secret that the vast majority of government elected and non-elected personnel are opposed to the Trump presidency. It requires no great stretch of the imagination to hypothesize government functionaries doing everything in their power to use the occasion of crudely implementing an early Trump executive order to sabotage his presidency. The fact that these bureaucrats applied the executive order without discretion and treated travelers as so many cattle does not justify the label of racist or Islamaphobe placed upon the head of Mr. Trump. If government functionaries and bureaucrats were truly interested in the American people, the security of the country, and doing their job to the best of their ability, they would have done everything in their power to smooth the rough edges of the early presidential transition period. They would have used their experience and common sense to keep processes running smoothly. Rather than do their jobs to the best of their abilities and serve the people traveling through American airports, they "worked to rule"[27] and did their best to throw a monkey wrench into the already extremely inefficient machinery of airport security and customs clearing for no other reason than to give the new president a black eye.

No one with any intelligence or common sense should expect that Mr. Trump will not have some difficulties adjusting to the way and lifestyle of the unique, dystopian world of Washington D.C. Many candidates make a pillar of their campaign the fact that they are less of a career politician, more of an outsider, than their opponent. Jimmy Carter won the presidency on just that primary qualification. Every third party candidate runs on that supposed limitation as an advantage. And in fact, this is precisely one of the qualities of Mr. Trump that so many millions of voters valued. He said he intended to "drain the swamp," to change the ultra-political, backstabbing, smoke-filled back room environment of D.C. and clear it of self-serving apparatchiks who use their power and influence to serve only themselves and their oligarchic friends at the expense of all others. This is precisely what most Americans want and it can only be done by someone who is not beholden to the entrenched powers in Mordor on the Potomic.

Is Mr. Trump a loose cannon? Is he somewhat crude in his speech and actions? Yes, and that's exactly what the American majority wants. In the government structure as originally envisioned by the founders, the public would not have such a direct influence on who was elected as president. Their design included intelligent, clear thinking, rational individuals choosing the chief officer of the

---

27 https://en.wikipedia.org/wiki/Work-to-rule

executive branch of the government. That has all but been replaced by popular plebiscite determined by sound bites and personality. Americans get the government they deserve, and they get it good and hard. Mr. Trump may not be in the tradition of Jefferson and Madison, but he is the result of the sway of extreme partisan politics of the twenty-first century.

Yeah, and so what? He believes late-term abortions, except in extreme cases to save the physical life of the mother, should be illegal. Other presidents have held the same view but they weren't treated as political pariahs. Mr. Trump has stated that, when presented the opportunity, he would appoint judges to the Supreme Court who hold his views. This is exactly the view of a majority of Americans, so to cry out that Mr. Trump is somehow desirous of turning back the clock in America is nonsense. In fact, history teaches us that as civilizations progress, abortion, infanticide, and other manifestations of cruelty and barbarity, of the lack of respect for human life decreases. Liberals adore democracy when it tilts their way. When it doesn't, it's "populism," it's the rise of the idiocracy, the "basket of deplorables" throwing a temper tantrum. But is not marching in the streets costumed like female genitalia[28] nothing more than demonstrating an inability to think and act rationally, throwing an immature, liberal temper tantrum?

Even though Mr. Trump has not yet appointed an anti-abortion Supreme Court justice, he did, on January 23, 2017 reinstate an executive order forbidding the payment of federal subsidies to specialized international nongovernmental associations (NGA's) that actively promote abortion. That seems pretty specifically aimed, no? This was nothing more than a warning to specific associations that they must make a choice: they can fulfil their social objective to help women, or accept funding from one of several of George Soros' organizations, organizations with the primary directive of bringing down

---

28 http://www.theblaze.com/news/2017/01/24/trans-community-womens-march-protesters-focus-on-female-genitalia-was-oppressive/

the Trump presidency and press forward toward a one-world government.[29] Mr. Trump's decree was not so much about abortion as avoiding another of Mr. Soros' "color revolutions." The executive order has been an on-again, off-again thing for years beginning with President Reagan. Democrat presidents cancel it, Republican presidents re-instate it. Mr. Trump is not saying the NGOs cannot promote abortions; he is saying they cannot operate with tax dollars from Americans who want no part of it.

The argument over abortion will never be resolved. Greek, Roman, and every civilization throughout history struggled with the question. It will also be noted by students of history that the more lenient the society became toward abortion, the less stable was the culture and the closer it was to its downfall. The issue involves, at its root, fundamental philosophical and religious questions that have been ongoing since the dawn of human history: When does human life begin? When does the soul enter the body? Does the body even have a soul? Does quality of life for one person outweigh the life of the other? These questions address the very meaning of life, the values, mores, and foundational spiritual beliefs of every culture. As long as we imbue the office of the president with an aura of spiritual and moral leadership, this and similar questions will continue. The U.S. populace will never allow a candidate to avoid stating his opinion on the subject of abortion. And once stated, the issue will be used to slice off a section of those who oppose his stance. Those people will then be solidly in the camp of the opponent, no matter the other issues.

---

29 http://dennismichaellynch.com/george-soros-words-aims-one-world-government/

There is no parallel to the issue of abortion. There is no analogous precedent to guide us. One side of the argument views the killing of a person who has harmed no one, no matter where that person may be in the life development process, as objectively wrong, as murder. On the other side are those who define "human" and "wrong" subjectively and say we need to take into consideration all the circumstances of the people who will be affected by the decision. They may look upon the unborn child as nothing more than excess tissue, no different from a cancer growth or a parasite that the host can eliminate at will with no consideration toward anyone but herself.

So the debate continues. But a candidate for president cannot *not* have an opinion on the subject; this would never be allowed. Whichever side of the fence he's on is going to be seen as unacceptable to a very vocal section of the voters. Mr. Trump is no different and his opinion on this question is not something that disqualifies him from holding office.

Even with that said, the president has very little control over the issue. He cannot make law; he can only enforce it. As noted above, were it not for the fact that the American people have imbued the office of the president with magisterial powers contrary to the highest law of the land that defines his duties of office, this would not even be an issue.

The fact that Mr. Trump does not support late-term abortions in no way disqualifies him from being the legitimate president of the United States and is certainly no reason for the vitriol thrown at him.

Mr. Trump's critics point to the fact that the Trump line of men's neckties are made in China even though he himself decries offshore manufacturing of American products. I can sympathize with the president on this point, as the same is said of libertarians—*You don't believe the government should build roads, yet you drive on them.* The reality is, if libertarians refuse to utilize government-provided resources in the world in which we live, we would simply not be able to live. Government presence is so all-encompassing it is impossible today to *not* interact with it and use the services it forces on us. Some of those services are useful. None are provided in the most efficient manner possible. In the same way, because of government regulations and policies, it is today impossible to manufacture many things in The United States and be competitive with the same products made in other countries. Donald Trump has stated, "That's the world we are living in. It's not a fantasy and it's not based on what you would like to happen." Mr. Trump's objective is to get American businesses in a position where they do not have to outsource manufacturing to not only stay competitive, but to simply stay in business.

In other words, we are all *forced* to play the game, to conform to government *diktates.* A person born in Thailand has to play the game of life created by the rules of Thai society and its government. In the same way, a person born within the borders of the United States must do the same with respect to his government and society. That doesn't mean that a person, with the right of free speech and the right to seek redress from his government can't ask for a rule change. Indeed, that's exactly what the twenty-seven amendments to the United States Constitution are all about; they are fundamental changes to the overarching original rules of the national government, and to which state and local governments must adhere.

Given a complete and thorough examination of our beliefs and actions, we are all forced to act hypocritically in one way or another every hour of every day. That's the price of living within a complex society. The less one interacts with others the less hypocritical one is forced to be. But a person who manages a multi-billion-dollar worldwide network of businesses is not allowed to run his affairs exactly as he might wish.

Mr. Trump is no different from anyone else in society in this respect. When one must act hypocritically to survive and thrive within civilization, that is no hypocrisy, but mere survival.

The fact that Donald Trump's actions in any visible manner—hiring, appointment of minorities to lead positions in his businesses and presidential campaign, and his social life—show no hint of racism doesn't stop the intelligentsia from discerning, in their unknown and unknowable way, what is truly going on in the mind of the man. Here's their claim in a nutshell. Trump is a racial instigator and he often answers accusations of racism by bellicosely protesting that he actually loves the group in question. This is *prima facie* evidence of racist views because he refers to people as part of a group, as in, "I have nothing against blacks."

But is that not how Social Justice Warriors and the liberal cognoscenti refer to protected classes, those *groups* of people who need special accommodation from their superior caretakers in every area of their lives? They say Trump treats racial groups as monoliths. But again, is this not exactly how their so-called defenders refer to them? How could there be hiring quotas for racial groups if they were not defined as having certain characteristics that placed them in a monolithic group? The Left attempts to avoid this dilemma by adding the noun "community" after the monolithic adjectival group name of Black, LGBTQ, Hispanic, Asian, etc., but this is just part and parcel of the games they play with words. Somehow saying, "I respect Black people," a racist statement according to the snowflake thought police of the SJW strain, is altogether different from "I respect the Black *Community,*" which is socially and politically acceptable. Saying "I have nothing against gays," or "I have friends who are gay" are both thinly veiled homophobic and bigoted statements according to the SJW's, while "I have friends in the Gay *Community*" is perfectly acceptable. Word play extends to our whole political vocabulary. When one has the support of liberal citizens, he or she is appealing to *democratic* ideals. Another person, appealing to conservatives, would be a vile *populist*. To believe in democracy (rule by popular consent) is good, but to be a populist (belief in rule by popular consent) is bad. Both express the concept of following the will of the majority in policy decisions, but when the will of the people goes the wrong way, when the popular sentiment is not in accord with the *more intelligent* will of the SJW's, that, then, is the evil of populism. When one appeals to liberal ideals, he is a *visionary*. Appealing to conservative ideals is *demagoguery*. "Person of Color" is just fine, while "colored person" is a racial epithet. The list goes on and on, with every day bringing a change to some word or phrase to suit the needs of the liberal, progressive class (liberal and progressive: two more words that have completely changed meaning over the last several decades.)

We have come to use words such as racist, bigot, homophobe, xenophobe, Nazi, fascist, and countless others to mean whatever we want them to mean at any time depending on their emotional impact. They are fluid, as so many think of a person's sexual identity. (Note, I didn't say gender—another word whose meaning has been forgotten.) Words with heavy emotional weight are bandied about as if they were nothing more than a general expletive, with no fixed definition other than to say the person referred to is a social pariah and a danger to civil society. The person referred to by any one or more of these words is to be feared and shunned by any rational, liberal, progressive member of polite society.

Word meanings do change over time. Nice originally meant lewd or wanton. Meat was used for anything one might eat for nourishment. A bully was a sweetheart of either sex. Fruition was the pleasurable use of something. Neat meant finely-dressed or without alteration. A clue was a ball of yarn or string. But these words have changed meaning slowly, over centuries. Figurative meanings became literal meanings, so clue, a ball of string that could be used to mark one's path through a maze to enable one to find the way out became the current word, clue, meaning an object that helps one to discover a solution or a way out of a mystery.

But referring to someone as homophobic, as someone who hates homosexuals or, by extension, is subconsciously fearful of his own repressed or subconscious homosexual tendencies and so is likely to lash out at those who reveal their homosexual bent, is disingenuous and simply wrong in the case of Donald Trump and so many millions of others in our society. One may hold the moral value that says practicing homosexual behavior is wrong, but that is in no way homophobic and holding to that moral code in no way suggests that person is likely to commit violence against someone who practices homosexual behavior. In the same way, referring to a woman who has had sex while inebriated and then has awakened the following day to regret it as the "victim" of "date rape" changes the meaning of the word rape and gives one no adequate word to describe the unlawful sexual activity, normally including sexual intercourse, *carried out forcibly or under threat of injury* against the will of a person.[30] At one time, before the memory of anyone living today, rape was defined as to seize (anything) and take away by force. Until very recently the meaning of the word was understood to include force and violence or the threat of violence against a person in order to engage in some sort of sexual activity. When we say a woman who wishes she hadn't gotten drunk and had

---

30 https://www.merriam-webster.com/

sex last night was "raped," what word are we to use to refer to what was done to the woman or man who was brutally attacked, forced to endure sexual intercourse, and then left for dead? When we use words like Nazi, fascist, bigot, and homophobe to mean whatever thought patterns or actions of which we disapprove, the words lose all meaning and leave us nothing to express the real thoughts behind those sounds.

When Sikhs prefer to socialize and form family relationships with other Sikhs do we say they are bigoted? When Jews prefer to socialize and form family relationships with other Jews are they bigoted or racist? When Black people prefer to socialize and form family relationships with other Blacks are they racist? Replace "European" or "white" with any of the adjectives in those three previous sentences. Suddenly, that person, indeed exemplifies the very definition of racist, bigoted, ethno centrist, and xenophobic.[31] These words no longer have a fixed meaning except as epithets against people of European descent. In effect, they have no meaning. Using them to describe President Trump is an exercise in meaninglessness because all meaning has been distilled from them by the liberal elites over the last several decades.

All that said, it ignores the fact that Mr. Trump has in fact never demonstrated actual racist tendencies, when racist is well-defined. His employment policies are not racist. No objective, intelligent person could infer racist tendencies from the mix of people in management positions in his companies and his campaign staff. The only way he can be referred to as a racist or bigot or homophobe is by redefining those words to their current meaningless state

---

31 This, in fact, points to a further problem: Only those of European descent, white people, if you will, are thought capable of the grave sins of discrimination, racism, and bigotry.

by the ultra-sensitive Social Justice Warriors who have co-opted the English language for their own purposes.

The undeniable fact is, most of what is printed and said about Donald Trump is profoundly hypocritical. Trump doesn't threaten gays, blacks, any minority, or any protected class. No honest person could say he's an anti-Semite, he is surrounded by Jewish family members and Jewish advisers. He is supported by the leaders of Israel. He is not anti-Muslim; the temporary travel restriction that he established early in his administration affects non-Muslims as well as Muslims entering the United States from a very limited number of countries, identified prior to his administration as regional sources of Islamist extremism. Only 109 travelers were detained during the confusion that resulted from the ban. In fact, it is not at all unreasonable to assume that the inconveniences and delays caused by the out-of-control *demonstrators* contributed more to the problems of travelers than the executive order itself. All this is to ignore the fact that Our Dear Leader President Obama also imposed a four-month travel ban on passengers from Iraq in 2011. Were there mass demonstrations against the Dear Leader's policies? A search of The New York Times, Washington Post, Huffington Post, and other mainstream media turns up nothing. How could that be?

By any objective, meaningful standard, Mr. Trump is not racist, bigoted, homophobic, anti-Semitic, or any of the other epithets so casually hurled against him.

Now we're getting to the root of what the Military-Industrial Complex and the Power Elite, the veiled oligarchical body that comprises the real power of the United States government is afraid of. Several weeks into the administration of Donald Trump, this seems, unfortunately, to be an unfounded fear. He has stated he believes the other member states should be forced to pay their dues and agreements with scofflaw nations are null and void until they pony up their fair share. Is this not an effective method of forcing the issue? Exactly why is enforcing a contract such an abhorrent thing? Mr. Trump stated during his campaign that NATO has possibly outlived its usefulness and our membership should be re-evaluated. Finally, a national figure not only recognizes but speaks the truth. NATO is a relic of the Cold War, a war that's been over since at least 1989. Would a reasoned discussion of the purpose of the organization and our continued membership in it, or of its continued existence be such a bad thing? This is what businesses do. A firm today engaged in the manufacture of buggy whips would be well-advised to reassess its strategy to determine whether it is putting its finances and creative energy into the most profitable arena. It's obvious that NATO's primary objective is not defensive, but offensive, and that the target is Russia, soon to be China. A defensive alliance against the U.S.S.R. may have been a good idea fifty years ago, but today it's nothing more than a holdover vestige of the past that can only serve to provoke a relatively peaceful nation. (Relative to the United States, a country that has been at war during 93% of its existence.[32])

Peaceful? But what about Ukraine? The Ukraine coup is a complex issue and deserves its own book. Suffice to say that there is ample reason and evidence to support the claim that the coup in Ukraine was sponsored and coordinated by the U.S. and Crimea—and again we find George Soros', Hillary Clinton's, and other American government fingerprints all over the evidence. Any student of history knows that Ukraine was part of Russia for almost as long as The United States has existed as a country and that over half its population is ethnic Russian.[33]

We also need to recognize the fact that if European nations were to pay their fair share for NATO and shoulder a proportionate burden of defending themselves militarily, the role of America as the Father Protector would be reduced along with its power to influence those countries' political processes. Indeed, the not-so-secret dirty little secret is that the U.S. *wants* to carry the lion's share of the cost of NATO. This is, in fact, a vital ingredient in pursuing and maintaining a unilateral world super-power status, one of the primary goals of the military-industrial-congressional complex in the United States.

The "war against terrorism" is a tool, a smokescreen to maintain an "orange" level of fear among a populous more concerned with Brangela and who gets to use which toilets at the mall. Fearful, distracted people are easy to control. In fact, creating the circumstances leading to fear is the

---

32 http://www.globalresearch.ca/america-has-been-at-war-93-of-the-time-222-out-of-239-years-since-1776/5565946
33 https://www.wilsoncenter.org/publication/why-did-russia-give-away-crimea-sixty-years-ago

prime *modus operandus* of governments worldwide and through history in maintaining control over the populace.

But wait, don't we have to maintain a strong alliance with other countries to fight terrorism?

Let's look at that. People pay for what's important to them. If you want to accurately assess someone's or some organization's values follow the money. Were the United States government really concerned with fighting terrorism, we'd see spending highly focused on the type of warfare engaged in by a loosely organized, underfunded enemy. If the American government were truly concerned with terrorism, we might see some convincing evidence that anyone really gives a shit about the root cause of the terrorist threat against the United States: the long and storied history of U.S. manipulation of Middle East politics and economics targeted against an opponent frozen in a middle-age mentality of religious warfare with Western civilization. But we see none of that. Rather, we see the primary expenditures of an ever-increasing military budget in grand weapons programs that can only be viewed as an arms buildup for war against other major states on the world scene—Russia and China.

- US Nuclear Weapon Upgrade Program: "CBO estimates that nuclear forces will cost $348 billion between FY 2015 and FY 2024. Three independent estimates put the expected total cost over the next 30 years at as much as $1 trillion."[34]
- The U.S Navy wants ten Gerald R. Ford-class aircraft carriers at a cost of $12.8 billion each, plus approximately $5 billion in R&D costs.

---

34 https://www.armscontrol.org/factsheets/USNuclearModernization

- The U.S. Air Force wants 175-200 B-21 nuclear-capable bombers at approximately $550 million per copy.
- The Navy wants a new fleet of Columbia-class nuclear submarines at a cost of $347 million.[35]

The list goes on and on. Each program benefits constituents of a number of powerful congress-critters. The efficacy of each program matters not. How many B-21 bombers and Columbia-class submarines does it take to stop one determined terrorist who believes paradise awaits him in return for mutilating himself and innocent others in jihad for his god?

The theory that President Reagan caused the downfall of the Soviet Union due to his build-up of military personnel and weapons systems, causing the bankruptcy of the U.S.S.R. as they attempted to maintain weapons parity while being hobbled by a failing economic system, continues to be the accepted root cause of the U.S. Cold War victory over the U.S.S.R. by those who accept the gospel according to the military-industrial-congressional complex. This is repeated and repeated *ad infinitum* by the mainstream media who are nothing more than said complex's house organ. They themselves know the myth of Reagan conquering the U.S.S.R. by outspending them to be just that, a myth. But they are confident that the U.S. population will continue to believe the myth and so will be willing to provide hundreds of billions of dollars, if not trillions, in taxed and borrowed funds to be thrown down the rat hole where sit, at the bottom, the very few who control the strings of the government puppet and who

---

35 https://en.wikipedia.org/wiki/Columbia-class_submarine#Overview

profit handsomely from the ignorance and fear of the American voters.

The only action better than forcing the member nations of NATO to cough up their fair share of the expenses of the organization would be to withdraw from the outdated, outmoded organization altogether. For promoting this idea, Mr. Trump should be praised.

This is only stated by people who are ignorant of the form of government of The United States of America and the process of electing the president in place since the adoption of the Constitution in 1789. The manner of electing persons to the offices of president and vice president was originally specified in Article II, Section 1, Paragraphs 2 and 3 of the Constitution. Paragraph 2 states:

> Each State shall appoint, in such Manner as the Legislature thereof may direct, a Number of Electors, equal to the whole Number of Senators and Representatives to which the State may be entitled in the Congress: but no Senator or Representative, or Person holding an Office of Trust or Profit under the United States, shall be appointed an Elector.

Paragraph 3 was superseded by the Twelfth Amendment, which reads:

> The Electors shall meet in their respective states, and vote by ballot for President and Vice-President, one of whom, at least, shall not be an inhabitant of the same state with themselves; they shall name in their ballots the person voted for as President, and in distinct ballots the person voted for as Vice-President, and they shall make distinct lists of all persons voted for as President, and of all persons voted for as Vice-President and of the number of votes for each, which lists they shall sign and certify, and transmit sealed to the seat of the government of the United States, directed to the President of the Senate;

Nowhere in the Constitution does it state that the president is elected directly by the individual persons of the various states. The Electoral College is not a relic of days gone by when forms of communication were slower and less efficient. Our system is the mechanism by which the (supposedly independent) states that comprise the union select the chief executive, the head of the executive branch, of the federal government. The executive branch is chartered to serve three principle functions: direct foreign affairs, coordinate military defense against other nations in time of *declared war*, and resolve disputes between the several (previously independent) states. The president was not intended to be the representative of individual citizens of the United States. That he has become so is an aberration of the system designed by the founders. That his role has become this, that this has been allowed to happen without Constitutional consideration, is the result of political games and institutional laziness on the part of Congress enabled by an ignorant voting populace.

> *How did we get here, after all? What is it that transformed the presidency from an unassuming "chief magistrate" to the unholy and unnatural amalgam of genie, warlord, and shaman that it has become? How have we arrived at our current predicament, in which we regularly entrust our hopes and dreams—as well as the world's most powerful military—to whichever professional office-seeker dissembles most convincingly on the campaign trail? What have we done to deserve this?*[36]

Were it not for the fact that we have vested the office of president with such unrealistic, utopian expectations we

---

36 Healy, Gene. The Cult of the Presidency (Cato Institute, 2008) p. 267 (first paperback printing, 2009)

wouldn't even be having this conversation. The president is supposed to be the chairman of the board of the executive branch of the federal government. He is not the leader of the free world. He is not the voice of the American people. He is not your or my president. He is simply the head of one branch of government who is supposed to have *very limited and defined powers*. Is his language somewhat course? If he can manage the affairs of the executive branch it shouldn't matter. Is he wealthy? If he can manage the affairs of the executive branch it shouldn't matter. Can he lead the country through times of tribulation? If he can manage the affairs of the executive branch that does not matter.

We may not be happy with what presidential politics offers us, but we're far from blameless. We demand a government that will solve all our problems but will also have the decency to leave us alone. We want a president who knows his place, but we also long for a leader who can transform crisis into opportunity, helping us realize our collective potential in a grand, national crusade. We want what we cannot have, and as a result, we get what we do not like.[37]

From another point of view, rather than view Mr. Trump as being illegitimate because he did not garner more individual votes than his opponent, it should be noted that he won the election in spite of a well-coordinated attack by his own political party and powerful individuals within elected and non-elected government. He also won in spite of his opponent's much larger campaign budget, vastly more numerous and experienced campaign staff, the well-known support of her party even in the primary process, overwhelming support of the press, and the political

---

37 Ibid.

capital built up over decades of political favors and intrigue behind her. By all rights, Donald Trump's election against all odds truly shows the will of the people, not just the "deplorables" as Hillary Clinton referred to his supporters.

This would not be an issue had the people of this country not, since roughly a century ago, grown increasingly desirous of a strong national leader. We have allowed a culture of virtual sainthood to inhabit the office of the president and constantly seek someone to fill the position who will act as the nation's moral and spiritual leader. As president, we want a king, pope, and father confessor combined into one holy, intelligent, handsome, well-spoken person. We want someone to comfort our afflictions, someone who feels our pain. He is expected to be present at the aftermath of local tragedies. We have created a cult of Americanism and the president is to lead it with all the charisma of the greatest of cult leaders through history and throughout the world.

In fact, presidents through history are rated not according to how well they do their job as specified in the Constitution, but how much they expand the authority and power of the office. Wartime presidents are consistently rated higher than those who serve during times of peace. In fact, a person who oversees the executive branch in times of peace and prosperity, who makes no obvious and successful power grab to aggrandize himself and the office of president is seen as a failure. Certainly Machiavelli and Nietzsche would agree, but is this the America we truly desire?

The election of 2016 indicated a sea change in American politics and society. The reason for the election's ensuing violence and vitriol is because the gulf between at least two distinct groups of people has become too wide to ignore any longer or to be rationally and peacefully reconciled. The president's supporters are, for the most part, the producers in American society. They are those who do useful things. They create, they add value to the lives of individuals, and they have grown increasingly frustrated and angry because they see those who feed off their productivity stifling their action while at the same time claiming a larger and larger portion of it in tribute, otherwise known as taxation. These are the people who build, engineer, manufacture, plant, grow, operate, maintain, repair, transport, and sell the things we find useful or essential.

The takers, the leeches on the productive class, the politicians and bureaucrats, those who produce nothing but instead only shuffle the paper of laws, rules, and regulations that slow and inhibit the productive class, depend on that class for their very jobs and income. Yet, for the most part they fail to realize they are killing the goose that lays their golden eggs. It seems that finally the productive class has concluded that continuing to support the political class in the manner to which they have become accustomed is no longer in their best interests.

Mr. Trump was the ideal candidate for very few people, but he was not a politician and he had demonstrated throughout his life that he was not a leech, that he actually created something that others would willingly buy. He hadn't spent his life forcing people under threat of violence to do that which they did not want, nor force them not to do that which they wanted. He offered trades they were free to accept or not *voluntarily* [38] . Therein lies the

---

[38] Yes, Trump took advantage of government rules, regulations, and programs that forced involuntary action by some. But again, he works within the legal bounds imposed on him by the government. See Screed Number Ten.

difference between Donald Trump and all his competitors in the campaign for president.

When the left says Donald Trump's presidency is "illegitimate," their real message is that our very desire for self-government is illegitimate. Donald Trump is merely a locus, an individual to focus on. Though he is wealthy, he is still able to represent the mundanes, those the elite, the intelligentsia, and the Social Justice Warriors truly think of as deplorables, those who dared to reject the rule of elites and demanded to finally be heard.

Boobus Americanus [39] seems to have its collective
underwear in a bundle over the question of whether some
geek in Russia hacked into a DNC network and stole emails.
Mr. Trump's opponents claim Russian agents hacked into
email servers of the Democratic National Committee and
released purloined communiques to Wikileaks
(https://wikileaks.org). The emails exposed the fact that
the Democratic National Committee (DNC) was aiding and
abetting the Clinton campaign and actively sabotaging that
of her main rival in the primary process, Bernie Sanders,
contrary to their stated purpose and rules they themselves
created. Clinton supporters claim this somehow damaged
her candidacy and helped the Trump campaign. If this
happened, someone on the other side of the globe is
responsible for shining a glaring beam of blinding, white
light on the DNC and their standard bearer, one Hillary
Rodham Clinton, and revealing her to be a devious,
scheming, lying, cheating, prevaricating, scumbag,
perfectly in tune with the rest of the DNC that was
supporting her during the entire primary process.

What, precisely, is Boobus Americanus upset about? Could
it be that the best the Democrat Party could put forward as
their candidate for president and leader of the free world
(sic) is in actuality the lowest of the low-life that inhabits
the hallowed halls of American government? Are they all
in a tither about the manipulation of party rules for the
benefit of HRC? Are they complaining about the
mainstream media that obviously and unabashedly

---

39 I am indebted to Butler Shaffer for coining this term.
https://lewrockwell.com/author/butler-shaffer/

supported her and trashed her opponent from the very beginning?

Hell no. They're angry that someone, and especially someone who isn't a citizen of this Shining Beacon on a Hill, let the public know exactly what a prevaricating, quibbling, dissembling Whore of Babylon their preferred presidential candidate actually is.

However, we now know that the CIA maintained an internal hacking program designed to imitate hackers based in Russia in order to create a false trail of evidence leading to that country. Even if actual Russian agents did hack into DNC servers, what explanation could there be for DNC and U.S. Security actions? We know in September of 2015 Special Agent Adrian Hawkins of the FBI informed the DNC, "At least one computer system belonging to the D.N.C. had been compromised by hackers federal investigators had named 'the Dukes,' a cyberespionage team linked to the Russian government." [40] The DNC accepted this information lightly, to say the least. Several weeks and several calls from the same FBI agent later, the DNC finally decided to call in a private contracting agency to investigate. Why did they not call in the FBI? Could it be because the DNC did not want the FBI to have access to emails they knew would be very embarrassing and would provide evidence of illegal activity?

Then-Director of the FBI, James Comey said, "The FBI requested direct access to the Democratic National Committee's (DNC) hacked computer servers but was denied." Another FBI official said, "The FBI repeatedly stressed to DNC officials the necessity of obtaining direct access to servers and data, only to be rebuffed until well

---

40 https://www.nytimes.com/2016/12/13/us/politics/russia-hack-election-dnc.html?_r=0

after the initial compromise had been mitigated." D.N.C. executives and their lawyers delayed their first formal meeting with senior F.B.I. officials for *nine full months*. A matter of grave national importance is delayed until it can do the most damage to the Democrat challenger? Folks, this just doesn't even pass the smell test.

Let's say, for sake of argument that agents of the Russian government did, in fact, hack into DNC computers. There is as yet no proof that the damaging emails in question were not simply given to Wikileaks by an insider within the DNC or the Clinton campaign who had an acute attack of conscience.

Turns out, that seems to be exactly what happened. On July 8, 2016, Seth Rich, a Democratic staffer, was murdered in Washington DC. The killer or killers took nothing from their victim, leaving behind his wallet with cash inside, watch, and phone.

It was reported shortly afterwards that Rich was en route to the FBI the morning of his murder, apparently intending to speak to special agents about an "ongoing court case" possibly involving the Clinton family. (Strange how so many people who were on the wrong side of the Clintons are no longer with us.) Then, in August of 2016 Wikileaks offered a $20,000 reward for information leading to the arrest and conviction of his killer. Julian Assange went so far as to suggest that Seth Rich was the Wikileaks informant.[41] This was confirmed by blogger Kim Dotcom who tweeted that he has evidence Seth Rich was the Wikileaks source, and stated that he is willing to release evidence to Congressional investigators.

---

41 https://twitter.com/Cernovich/status/763166970569224193

Yes, CIA and FBI spokespeople still say the leaked emails were the result of computer hacking, but no proof has been shown and we know for a fact that, in general, government functionaries lean heavily toward the Democrat Party, and the CIA is deeply embedded in what used to be called the Military-Industrial Complex, now known as the Deep State. In a congressional Intelligence Subcommittee hearing held March 20, 2017, FBI Director James Comey reported, after eight months of investigation of the leaked emails of the Clinton campaign and related matters, there is no evidence of collusion between Mr. Trump or his campaign staff and Russia. The former Director of National Intelligence General James Clapper, as of the same date, stated he agrees with Mr. Comey's statement. Ex-acting CIA Director Mike Morrell has stated, "On the question of the Trump campaign conspiring with the Russians here, there is smoke, but there is no fire, at all. ... There's no little campfire, there's no little candle, there's no spark."

While no collusion between Trump and Russia has been found, what has been discovered through the investigation is that there is collusion between the U.S. government's intelligence community and the news sources decidedly and obviously in favor of and supportive of another Clinton presidency. As reported by columnist Patrick Buchanan,[42] both "news" outlets were beneficiaries of illegal leaks.

Almost completely ignored was the evidence from the leaked emails that the DNC actively sabotaged the Sanders campaign and the underhanded methods of the DNC during the entire primary process. Rather, the leak was used by the Clinton campaign and her presstitute media supporters to demonstrate Russia favored a Trump win.

---

42 https://www.lewrockwell.com/2017/03/patrick-j-buchanan/backfire-left/

Ms. Clinton's stand concerning action against Syria indicated a firm willingness to provoke war with Russia while Mr. Trump stated repeatedly during his campaign that he would prefer to diplomatically work out American and Russian differences. Can any intelligent person question why political leaders of Russia would prefer Trump to Clinton?

And why, exactly, would any intelligent, rational, discerning person find harm in the fact that the populace of this fair country might be in possession of more rather than less information about a presidential candidate? If ignorance is bliss, we can only deduce that Boobus Americanus prefers blissful ignorance to the uncomfortable vicissitudes of life.

They're not angry that their candidate is a scumbag, that she got caught with her hand in the cookie jar, that she's the only one standing in front of the burning house with a burnt match in one hand and an empty gas can in the other. They're only upset that she was *outed* as a scumbag, that she was photographed pouring the gas. They don't care that she's responsible for the deaths of hundreds of thousands of people in far off countries on the other side of the globe. No, the important fact, the one salient fact that rises above all else is that she's a woman, and it's time the United States had a president with a vagina and breasts, dammit! The fact that this candidate was one of the worst people to ever throw her hat in the ring for consideration of the esteemed office has no bearing on the matter. Half the voting populace wanted a woman in the office and they would have supported Lizzie Borden herself if she had been the Democratic Party candidate.

To Boobus Americanus, style beats substance any day of the week.

This is precisely the problem with democracy. There will always be more people of average and below intelligence than those at the higher end of the intellectual spectrum. Given the complexity of the world today, allowing Boobus a part in the selection of leadership is bound to be fraught with error and bad judgment.[43]

We, the majority, don't want to be forced to make calculated, rational decisions. The time required to sort through the information available and educate oneself in vital issues of the day takes time away from *American Idol* and *The Voice* and *Real Housewives* and baseball, basketball, and football and professional beach volleyball and pro skateboarding... This is why we are, for the most part, perfectly comfortable making life-changing decisions based on a very limited set of categories we can "wrap our heads around." Is this candidate in favor of at-will abortion at any stage of pregnancy? Yes? Then I'm for her. Is this candidate pro-second amendment? Yes? Then I'm for him. It's difficult to be informed and to weigh pros and cons of important issues, to consider future ramifications of policy. So, we don't.

Is Donald Trump a Russian patsy? The assertion is absurd on its face and becomes more so the more a rational, intelligent person looks at the evidence.

---

43 For much more on this see Democracy: The God That Failed. Hoppe, Hans Herman. Transaction Publishers, July, 2001

In the 60's, when presidents, candidates for the office, or those calling for massive social reform sufficiently threatened the *military-industrial complex*, now morphed into the *military-industrial-congressional-security complex* and what is better termed the *Deep State*, they were taken out by the most direct means possible: assassination. Of course we refer here to John and Robert Kennedy, Martin Luther King, and others lesser known. The powers of the Deep State know this is no longer an option; the information available through alternative news sources via the internet is much too broad, deep, and quickly delivered to attempt such a grand show again. While they maintain control of the mainstream media, they have lost the total control they enjoyed and exercised during the 60's and 70's.

This time around a bloodless coup is in order. The political assassination of Donald Trump began the day it became apparent he had any chance at all to win the Republican nomination for presidential candidate. The greatest threat against Mr. Trump is the critters at the bottom of the rat hole, the Deep State that never wanted him in office in the first place. Hillary Clinton or Jeb Bush would have been perfectly acceptable to them, but Donald Trump spoke to the concerns of the majority of Americans and had enough money of his own to mount a successful candidacy. The fact that Donald Trump actually went on to win the presidency won't stop them. They own the media, the banks, and the influential think tanks which are in reality nothing more than propaganda dissemination centers run by the Washington intelligentsia. The soft coup happening at present will continue until Mr. Trump is either impeached and convicted or otherwise forced to resign from office. All the Social Justice Warriors who are crying about his bad words and clumsy rhetoric are nothing more than Useful Idiots. [44] They're being played by the Deep State to help push Donald Trump from office, to be replaced by someone they can control. Mike Pence comes to mind. Their purpose is continued manipulation of the economy and continued enrichment of themselves.

The Deep State can make this happen because they know from years of practice exactly what types of information to feed the public, exactly what will pull at the heart strings and resonate perfectly in synch with the decades of anti-liberty, anti-business propaganda hundreds of millions of Americans have been fed through the government-controlled school system and major media. They know how to appeal to the emotions of the left-leaning booboisie, and they know that emotions are the only thing to which they need appeal.

The Left, the cognoscenti, the elites don't merely disagree with Middle America. They don't feel those who value the Judeo-Christian heritage of this country are simply misinformed. No, in a word, they hate us.

And forget about "Love trumps hate." According to millions of anti-trumpers, if it would have been acceptable to assassinate Hitler prior to 1939, then it is equally acceptable to use physical violence, even to the extent of calling for the assassination of the president to rid the world of the "evil" of Donald Trump. Celebrities make such comments, comedians make jokes about it, and the mainstream media says nothing. Were the shoe on the other foot, had Hillary won the presidency and anyone joked about assassination, much less had anyone said the slightest serious word hinting at the act, the New York Times would make headlines of it and the government

---

44 https://en.wikipedia.org/wiki/Useful_idiot

would prosecute such persons as domestic terrorists and lock them up for life. The left won't readily or publicly admit it, but if violence propels their agenda, then violence there will be. And the government, evidenced by that of UC Berkeley police in April 2017, will stand by and let it happen. Is it not apparent that the government of California gives full approval of the use of violence against the conservative mundanes?

Donald Trump's Policies Should Be Examined

All that is not to say that Mr. Trump does not pose serious threats to the traditions of America. During an interview in late 2015, Mr. Trump let his authoritative side be known when he said he tends to "err on the side of security." He also stated that he believes parts of the PATRIOT Act that have been weakened by amendment should be restored. The rights of Americans are being slowly but inexorably eroded. This began during the War for Southern Independence when freedom was curtailed as a temporary war measure. But government action takes place with a ratchet that only works in one direction. Whatever leverage the government can use to increase its power and authority over the citizens and economic activity of the country is used, and that authority is never significantly relinquished. Sure, small, insignificant powers will be given up on occasion to give Boobus-Americanus the impression that the government is actually concerned with and protecting the freedoms of the citizenry, but for the greater part the power and authority of the government ratchets up and is never released.

Again, during World War I and then through the depression government took greater control and the citizens found themselves with less freedom. One couldn't even grow grain to feed one's own livestock on one's own farm without the federal government claiming the right to regulate it.[45] World War Two brought yet more controls and oversight over personal freedom and every trace of economic activity that could be discovered and the rate of dissolution of American's birthright of freedom has been increasing steadily. Mr. Trump doesn't seem to have a problem with this.

On the slightly positive side, from the point of view of personal liberty, even though he did not vacate the unconstitutional office of secretary of Education, he has at least appointed a weak head.

He has also continued the unconstitutional Environmental Protection Agency, although as head he has appointed someone who at least seems to take a rational view of EPA policies and the theory of human caused global climate change. He has withdrawn the United States from the Paris Climate Change Accords but has left open the possibility of instituting new talks.

However, while he stated famously that he intended to "drain the swamp," his appointments, for the most part, have shown he is too willing to select as advisors neo-conservatives whose hallmark is the desired expansion of American economic and military power throughout the world and a heavier military hand even within the borders of the United States. It seems we have business as usual on the military-industrial front, as Mr. Trump has just committed to allow Saudi Arabia, a country known to

---

45 http://sites.gsu.edu/us-constipedia/wickard-v-filburn-1942/

85

support world-wide terrorism, to purchase $110 million worth of arms from the U.S.[46]

Possibly, Mr. Trump believes he has to engage certain power centers in Washington D.C. in order to have any hope of accomplishing anything at all. But at this point in his administration, five months gone, he has shown no serious effort to drain anything and even Mr. Trump's supporters have to acknowledge and deal with his authoritarian tendencies.

He tweeted that anyone who burns the flag should face consequences. This seems odd, since he was willing to admit that the issue of same sex marriage has been adjudicated by the Supreme Court. Likewise, flag burning has been judged by SCOTUS as an issue of free political speech and is now a non-issue vis-à-vis the federal government.

High tariffs and protectionist trade policies are tools of government that have been proven throughout history to be not only useless toward the goal of overall economic advancement, but counter-productive. Tariffs may help the very narrow interests of a specific industry and constituency, but they never help the common man and they never aid general economic growth.

While Mr. Trump claims to be a supporter of the right of self-protection, he also supports taking away a person's right to self-defense with a firearm under no more than suspicion—being on a government watch list. This is further evidence of his extreme authoritarianism. Anyone can end up on a watch list and not even know it. One

---

46 http://www.independent.co.uk/news/world/americas/donald-trump-arms-deal-saudi-arabia-110-billion-911-terrorism-international-law-war-crimes-a7747076.html

doesn't have to be charged with anything, much less have been arrested and convicted. Once one finds himself on a watch list, which evidence may be denial of boarding an airplane or denial of the right to purchase a firearm, the onus to prove innocence is on the individual; appeal is expensive, time consuming, and beyond the ability of most citizens. This only underscores the problem that due process has been steadily eroded since 9/11. Mr. Trump seems not to have any problem with this.

Most Americans welcomed his belief that in his position as president he should place America's interests first. But an *extreme* nationalism is not only detrimental to the liberty of citizens, but can easily be seen by people of other nations and their governments as threatening, resulting in an increased level of fear that then results in greater government control. Respecting the individual rights of life, liberty, and the pursuit of happiness, regardless of where one may live in the world, would demonstrate this nation's dedication to benign governance that would indicate we intend no harm to anyone, and that the American government does not want to micro-manage its own citizens, much less the governments and citizens of other countries.

During a campaign appearance in Ft. Dodge, Iowa, Mr. Trump as a candidate said he would "...*bomb the shit out of*" the Islamic State (AKA ISIS). "I'd blow up every single inch, there would be nothing left. We'll get Exxon to come in there and in two months ... I'll take the oil..." He said he'd hit ISIS and kill their family members. He also said that he would institute a program of torture for suspected terrorists that goes beyond what went on in the Bush II administration. So far, he's fulfilling his campaign promise on drone strikes, and heaven only knows at this point if he's increasing the use of torture. The frequency of drone strikes has increased even from the profligate level of his predecessor. According to *Airwars*, a British monitoring group, alleged civilian casualties linked to U.S. strikes in Syria and Iraq were 1,472 in March, 2017. In March 2016, 196 civilians were reported killed. The previous high for any single month was 613. Many people who voted for him were hoping for a more reasoned foreign (AKA, war) policy. Using a sledge hammer to swat at mosquitoes in your dining room is likely to cause significant domestic damage, even if you do manage to hit the mosquito. Further, we know that killing of terrorists and their families just creates more terrorists. The country needs a more reasoned and rational approach to the tactic of terrorism directed against Americans and other people around the world. We simply cannot stop terrorism by killing terrorists. For every one the military or CIA kills, ten more appear to replace him. The problem of terrorism is not created by a finite number of bad people in the world; it is created by a powerful military and government who seek to impose controls over the sovereignty of other people and nations when those nations have no other way of fighting back. Terrorism is a tactic of warfare, nothing more nor less. Retribution for a million-dollar missile is easily accomplished by $500 worth of explosives and a single person willing to give up his life.

Again, this does not address the fundamental problem of a violent Islamist mentality intent on conquering the world for Allah and Muhammed. You don't improve the situation of a hornet's nest in your neighbor's back yard by constantly poking it with a stick.

This is to say nothing of the idea of Exxon coming in after the U.S. military has temporarily blown away the opposition. Mr. Trump's detractors have called him a fascist, but normally they use the term in a manner that demonstrates their ignorance of the word's true meaning. For most of them, fascist is a catch-all term for anyone they don't like. What they're normally saying is that he's anti-Muslim, anti-women, anti-Jew, that he wants to "turn back the clock" on American society. As I've shown above, none of these accusations are accurate or contain any truth. However, true fascism is a form of radical authoritarian nationalism characterized by dictatorial power, forcible suppression of opposition, *and state control of* [nominally private] *industry and commerce.* Mr. Trump has not "forcibly suppressed" his opposition yet, but has stated in an interview with WFOR, CBS' Miami affiliate, that he believes the First Amendment provides too much protection and he'd like to change the laws to make lawsuits against media companies easier. Trump said under current law, "our press is allowed to say whatever they want," implying that that's a bad thing. More worrisome, though are statements to the effect that corporate partners, e.g., Exxon, are going to work in partnership with the government to conquer enemies abroad and take their assets. This certainly leans toward the dictionary definition of fascism. Trump's authoritarian streak and extreme nationalism combine to give one reason to be concerned that the growing arrangement of government-business partnership will be strengthened under his administration.

Unfortunately, this presents a true problem only for libertarians and others who are deeply concerned with the growth of government and the diminution of personal liberty. Both progressive and conservative camps find a government-business partnership perfectly acceptable. In fact, the United States has been moving toward the dictionary definition of fascism for some decades. The pace has only increased since 9/11. The only questions today are, which businesses are controlled and to what extent? Progressives push for the government-health care industry partnership. Conservatives, on the other hand, see nothing wrong with partnerships among armaments manufacturers and energy companies. Both sides welcome the increasing security state, even though they want to use it for dissimilar purposes. Neither side will admit to the fact that a partnership between industry and a government that controls society through the threat and use of violence is antithetical to the liberty of the citizens of the nation.

Mr. Trump seems to see nothing wrong with the ideas of asset forfeiture imposed on those who have not been convicted of a crime or the use of imminent domain that allows government bodies to seize property for any use. This all points to authoritarianism that was one of the key ingredients of the regime Americans overthrew in 1776.

For all of Mr. Trump's faults, the American public was given a choice between him and a candidate who was much worse. We are where we are not because of the faults of the candidates, but because of the faults of the American public, which is in truth nothing more than the faults of the human race. Given a choice, most people will work less rather than more. Given a choice, most people will accept handouts over working for everything they receive. Given a choice, most people will follow a strong, dynamic leader rather than thoughtfully consider the state of the world around them and make prudent, intelligent decisions regarding their long term welfare. Most human beings want a king; we want to be led, and we don't really care much where we're led, as long as we don't have to take point and make difficult decisions. We want the easy route, the path already blazed, and we want someone to blame when things don't go well.

Politicians take advantage of our human frailty. In a democracy we get the government we deserve, and we get it good and hard. If nothing else, we can count on the Trump presidency to delay the process of the United States being subsumed into a one-world government; we can maintain the hope that we maintain some sovereignty in the world for another several years. The fact that this will come with stifled economic growth and the creation of even more enemies around the world is the price we'll have to pay for desiring a strongman at the helm and for allowing ourselves, as a nation, to be led into a swamp from which there is no likely exit short of economic and social catastrophe.

Chief Justice Roberts, President Carter, President Clinton, President Bush, fellow Americans, and people of the world, thank you.

We the citizens of America have now joined a great national effort to rebuild our county and restore its promise for all our people.

Together we will determine the course of America for many, many years to come.

Together we will face challenges. We will confront hardships. But we will get the job done.

Every four years we gather on these steps to carry out the orderly and peaceful transfer of power.

And we are grateful to President Obama and First Lady Michelle Obama for their gracious aid throughout this transition. They have been magnificent, thank you.

Today's ceremony, however, has very special meaning because today we are not merely transferring power from one administration to another – but transferring it from Washington DC and giving it back to you the people.

For too long a small group in our nation's capital has reaped the rewards of government while the people have borne the cost.

Washington flourished but the people did not share in its wealth. Politicians prospered but the jobs left and the factories closed.

The establishment protected itself but not the citizens of our country.

Their victories have not been your victories. Their triumphs have not been your triumphs. While they have celebrated there has been little to celebrate for struggling families all across our land.

That all changes starting right here and right now because this moment is your moment. It belongs to you. It belongs to everyone gathered here today and everyone watching all across America today.

This is your day.

This is your celebration.

And this – the United States of America – is your country.

What truly matters is not what party controls our government but that this government is controlled by the people.

Today, January 20 2017, will be remembered as the day the people became the rulers of this nation again.

The forgotten men and women of our country will be forgotten no longer. Everyone is listening to you now.

You came by the tens of millions to become part of a historic movement – the likes of which the world has never seen before.

At the center of this movement is a crucial conviction—that a nation exists to serve its citizens.

Americans want great schools for their children, safe neighborhoods for their families and good jobs for themselves.

These are just and reasonable demands

Mothers and children trapped in poverty in our inner cities, rusted out factories scattered like tombstones across the landscape of our nation.

An education system flushed with cash, but which leaves our young and beautiful students deprived of all knowledge. And the crime and the gangs and the drugs which deprive people of so much unrealized potential.

We are one nation, and their pain is our pain, their dreams are our dreams, we share one nation, one home and one glorious destiny.

Today I take an oath of allegiance to all Americans. For many decades, we've enriched foreign industry at the expense of American industry, subsidized the armies of other countries, while allowing the sad depletion of our own military.

We've defended other nations' borders while refusing to defend our own.

And spent trillions and trillions of dollars overseas while America's infrastructure has fallen into disrepair and decay.

We have made other countries rich while the wealth, strength and confidence of our country has dissipated over the horizon.

One by one, shutters have closed on our factories without even a thought about the millions and millions of those who have been left behind.

But that is the past and now we are looking only to the future.

We assembled here today are issuing a new decree to be heard in every city, in every foreign capital, in every hall of power – from this day on a new vision will govern our land – from this day onwards it is only going to be America first – America first!

Every decision on trade, on taxes, on immigration, on foreign affairs will be made to benefit American workers and American families.

Protection will lead to great prosperity and strength. I will fight for you with every bone in my body and I will never ever let you down.

America will start winning again. America will start winning like never before.

We will bring back our jobs, we will bring back our borders, we will bring back our wealth, we will bring back our dreams.

We will bring new roads and high roads and bridges and tunnels and railways all across our wonderful nation.

We will get our people off welfare and back to work – rebuilding our country with American hands and American labor.

We will follow two simple rules – buy American and hire American.

We see good will with the nations of the world but we do so with the understanding that it is the right of all nations to put their nations first.

We will shine for everyone to follow.

We will reinforce old alliances and form new ones, and untie the world against radical Islamic terrorism which we will eradicate from the face of the earth.

At the bed rock of our politics will be an allegiance to the United States.

And we will discover new allegiance to each other. There is no room for prejudice.

The bible tells us how good and pleasant it is when god's people live together in unity.

When America is united, America is totally unstoppable.

There is no fear, we are protected and will always be protected by the great men and women of our military and most importantly we will be protected by god.

Finally, we must think big and dream even bigger. As Americans, we know we live as a nation only when it is striving.

We will no longer accept politicians who are always complaining but never doing anything about it.

The time for empty talk is over, now arrives the hour of action.

Do not allow anyone to tell you it cannot be done. No challenge can match the heart and fight and spirit of America. We will not fail, our country will thrive and prosper again.

We stand at the birth of a new millennium, ready to unlock the mysteries of space, to free the earth from the miseries of disease, to harvest the energies, industries and technologies of tomorrow.

A new national pride will stir ourselves, lift our sights and heal our divisions. It's time to remember that old wisdom our soldiers will never forget, that whether we are black or brown or white, we all bleed the same red blood of patriots.

We all enjoy the same glorious freedoms and we all salute the same great American flag and whether a child is born in the urban sprawl of Detroit or the windswept plains of Nebraska, they look at the same night sky, and dream the same dreams, and they are infused with the breath by the same almighty creator.

So to all Americans in every city near and far, small and large, from mountain to mountain, from ocean to ocean – hear these words – you will never be ignored again.

Your voice, your hopes and dreams will define your American destiny.

Your courage, goodness and love will forever guide us along the way.

Together we will make America strong again, we will make America wealthy again, we will make America safe again and yes – together we will make America great again.

Thank you.

God bless you.

And god bless America.

Part Two: Random Thoughts on What I Think I Know So Far

INTRODUCTION

Over the last few years I posted most of the following articles to a blog site, *Random Anarcho-Capitalist Thoughts* (RandomACThoughts.Blogspot.com). The better-read articles had, I believe, maybe sixty to seventy hits. Self-promotion is not my strong point. So, assuming you have not seen these, an assumption I assume to be completely safe, I reprint them here for your enjoyment.

Full disclosure: On my more conservative days I'm a libertarian. When I'm feeling really radical, I'm more of an anarchist, but an anarchist in the original sense of the word, from Greek, *anarchos,* meaning having no ruler. In this guise, "ruler" may be thought of as the State, that organization that holds itself together by threatening anyone within its borders with some level of violence, even violence leading to death, if they don't behave (as defined by the State). I don't reject governance, *per se*; there always needs to be governance for a society to function and individuals must govern themselves. But individuals and societies can be governed by methods other than a State which arrogates unto itself the power and authority to impose its rules under threat of violence. The methods by which this has been and continues to be done is outside of the scope of this small book. Check the bibliography for references.

WHAT GIVES YOU THE RIGHT?

Have you ever asked yourself what gives you the moral right to do what you do? For example, what gives you the right to take from someone the fruits of his labor without his consent? You may reply, "Justin, don't be ridiculous. That would be theft. I don't have the right to steal from anyone." Of course, I agree. Let's rephrase the question. What gives you the right to delegate the right or hire someone to take from another the fruits of his labor without his consent? Again, you tell me you have no right to ask or expect anyone to do what is plainly illegal. But what if you take a vote among your neighbors and 51% of them vote in a fair and democratic plebiscite to take your neighbor's Mercedes and share it among yourselves? Again, you say you don't have that right. You're probably beginning to see a pattern by now. Let's continue. You put an initiative on a city-wide ballot, following all applicable rules and regulations, which, if approved by at least 51% of eligible voters, will give you and your neighbors the right to take your neighbor's Mercedes to share among yourselves. I've struck out again—you're going to tell me again you don't have the right to do that.

I believe that if I progress to a large enough group of people, let's say the entire state you live in, to vote for the measure, I'll eventually get you to say that you do indeed have that right. After all, now we're talking Democracy, the secular god of the Western World. I posit that the reality of the situation is this: You vote for a representative to place before his friends in Congress a bill that, if passed, will take the *money* from your neighbor that he might have used to pay for a Mercedes. Or he may have used it to pay for college for his daughter, or take a vacation, or help fund his retirement, or pay for medical care for his elderly mother, or whatever other thing he would prefer to do with his own hard-earned money, his own property. You feel that your idea for how he should use his money, if you can get a majority of others to agree with you, is superior to your neighbor's opinion of what to do with it. Therefore, you have the right within a democratic society to take it from him.

Every time we vote for a representative in a government body that has the power, under threat of violence, to take from others the fruits of their labors we are stealing from them, plain and simple. And again I ask, what gives you the moral right?

You might respond that that's democracy, the greatest political system ever invented by man. Or as Winston Churchill said, Democracy is the worst system of government, except for all the others.

I'd have to disagree. Democracy can be illustrated by two wolves and a sheep voting on what to have for dinner. Or, to put a crude spin on it, democracy might best be graphically illustrated by a gang rape. Democracy has nothing to do with natural rights and in fact is not better than any other political system for protecting human rights. According to Hans Herman-Hoppe, democracy has proved itself to be wholly inadequate to the task and has been a root cause of what might be the most horrible century in the history of mankind as measured by war, misery, and destruction of property, society, and lives.[47]

Democracy gives millions of people the justification to do things they would never think of doing by themselves. But somehow that action becomes perfectly acceptable when the authority for it, which never existed among any of the

---

[47] Hans Hermann Hoppe. Democracy: The God That Failed. See Bibliography for full citation.

individuals, is delegated via the religion of democracy to someone else. But a right you do not hold individually cannot be delegated to someone else or a group. I can't personally threaten someone at gunpoint and take half of his income to spend on what I think is a better use of that money, no matter the use. But through the magic of democracy, I and 51% of others within a population arbitrarily selected by others under the control of a State can hire (with money stolen from others) people with guns (police, Treasury agents, and countless other government officials) to threaten those who do not comply with our desires to relinquish the fruits of their labors. We can also force them to associate with people we would like them to associate with, to do business with people we want them to do business with, or rent or sell their privately-owned property to those to whom we want them to rent or sell, or any number of other actions that a majority votes for. In fact, I cannot and would not personally do any of those things myself, knowing that I have no moral right to do so. But suddenly, with democracy as my shield, I can legally do horrific things to others because I have convinced fifty-one percent of people within my political sphere to agree to do them, or to vote for someone who will authorize the action to be carried out by people in State-issued uniforms and who carry guns.

With democracy, you can have the legal right to do these things, but again I ask, where do you get the moral right and the moral authority? What gives you the moral authority to authorize others to steal for you? Keep people apart who would like to be together? Keep people together who would prefer to be apart? To kill people who have never threatened you? To do any number of things or prohibit the same number of things with the tens of thousands of laws and regulations, the extent of which *not one person* on the face of the Earth can possibly know or understand?

You might answer, "That's just how things are. Someone has to make the rules. Someone has to decide what we can and can't do. That's what maintains an orderly society. We all have certain rules we have to live with. We can't just all do what we want."

Imagine yourself two hundred years ago as a plantation owner when a slave might ask, "Who gives you the moral authority to shackle me and force me to do your bidding? To take from me the fruits of my labors? To keep me from the people I love? You would tell him, "That's just how things are. Someone has to make the rules. Someone has to decide what we can and can't do. That's what maintains an orderly society. We all have certain rules we have to live with. We can't all just do what we want."

I suggest it's time to start imagining a different way. We might not all think we're living in the best of all possible worlds, but we accept the injustices and crimes committed in our names, thinking that this is just the price of civilization. We'll make it better when we finally vote in the representatives of *our* party, those good, honest, and forthright people who will finally right all wrongs and put society on the path to perfection.

It's time we woke up and smelled the coffee. Government parties have changed, philosophies of governments have changed, the players on the world's government stages have changed, but the institution of government itself has continued to grow and take more and more power. The government's schools teach millions of people that the form of democracy in these United Sates is the best of all possible worlds and we have to support our government no matter what. Not only that, but we have to force our form of democracy on other countries and cultures, even at gunpoint, because the end justifies the means. And the end is control of the people of the world by The United States government.

And all the while, no one seems to ask, what gives you the right?

I Don't Support the Troops

I have to say at the outset that "not supporting the troops" in no way implies that I have any ill will against any one person in the military. On the contrary, I have no ill will against anyone, which is one of the reasons I don't "support the troops." Still people will look for insult and justification for taking offense wherever they can find it. If I say I do not support the U.S. troops spread around the world, there will certainly be people who will take extreme offense hold with the former President Bush who believes, "You're either with us or against us." The absurdity and childishness of that statement deserves its own article, so I won't say any more about it here.

Not supporting the troops means I do not give them moral support and would withhold financial support if it were within my power to do so. Given the choice, I would not contribute in any way to their continued presence and actions outside the borders of this country unless we were attacked by the military of another country, and then I would voluntarily join the fight with my own guns to protect hearth and home. But I do not support the millions of personal, individual decisions that have led to millions of U.S. Troops having been and continuing to be in Middle East countries and over one hundred other countries around the world where the U.S. Empire has a military presence.

I have friends and relatives in the military. Some have lost their lives to what they believed to be service to their country. I feel bad that their lives were wasted, but that does not equate to support for their actions. I feel incredible sadness that hundreds of thousands of lives have been wasted on the hegemonic policies of The United States, and my heart goes out to their families and friends.

But, this does not translate into a reason to support the troops in any manner. At present, they should not be wherever they are outside of the borders of the United Sates.

There are people who agree with everything I have said, but who still believe everyone should support the troops on principal alone. "My country, right or wrong." But if I should support the troops on principle, simply because I was born within the borders of the United States, then shouldn't it follow, logically, that *all* citizens of *all* countries in *all* times should support their troops? A principle is, by definition, something you hold to come hell or high water, and holds in all circumstances. Therefore, to say that, in principle, the citizens of a country should support their troops is to say that Germans should have supported the SS and others who were rounding up Jews, homosexuals, Gypsies, and all other undesirables as defined by the legal, legitimate German government of the time and working them to death in forced labor camps and slaughtering those deemed useless in death camps. You might respond that these troops were engaged in illegal and immoral activities, so they are not deserving of the people's support. And "legal" is a concept defined solely by the government, so their acts were certainly legal. But what is morals is a very fluid concept. If your morals allow you to support the troops, that is your prerogative. But if your morals tell you to support the troops, and at the same time tell you that what they are doing is wrong, then there needs to be reconciliation between those conflicting concepts of morality. Resolution of internal conflict is where one must fall back to principles, and my principles do not support U.S. troops committing murder and mayhem and destroying property and families around the globe for any reason. Any act of aggression against a person in another country who has never posed a threat to any person in this country is clearly and unavoidably immoral. The presence of the military in Afghanistan, Iraq, Pakistan, and even South Korea, Germany, Japan, and the other 130 countries in six of the seven continents on this Earth where U.S. troops are present is illegal by the highest law of the land and flies in the face of the principles of the founders of this country.

Certainly I can't compare the American troops in Afghanistan, Pakistan, Iraq, and other outposts of the American Empire with Nazis and the Japanese army of World War II?

No, although Abu Graib and the CIA "rendition" and torture practices might allow one to debate even that. But for my argument, it's not necessary to compare the U.S. troops to Nazis. It is only necessary to make the point that if I, as one born within the borders of the United States, should support the troops in principle simply because of where I was born and happen to be a citizen, then others should support the troops of their countries in principle, without thought of the morality or justness of their actions.

But that is patently false. Wrong is wrong, and evil is evil. We do not owe support to that with which we disagree or find distasteful or morally abhorrent. There is no logical basis for saying, "I don't support what they are doing but I support the individuals." Each individual person is responsible for his or her own actions. Every person in the military today is a volunteer. Every person has access to the information that the U.S. has been involved in more wars than any country in modern history. Every citizen should know that the United States government has directly overthrown at least thirteen sovereign governments since 1898.[48]

There is no question that the United States today is, in practical terms, an empire and will stop at nothing to extend its power and influence anywhere in the world for the benefit of the corporations and banks that provide the campaign contributions that keep the politicians in office and provide their lavish lifestyle. Everyone serving in the military today has access to the history of this country and can read the Constitution and judge for himself whether he wants to involve himself in the struggle for U.S. global hegemony.

If it is an individual's belief that these actions are morally correct or justified and he decides to take part in the on-going expansion of the U.S. Empire and U.S. meddling in the political and economic decisions of other countries, that is his decision. But I will not. And I should not be expected to ignore my morals and convictions and support the troops in their extra-constitutional actions.

I will, however, support each and every troop who lays down his gun, refuses to push the launch button, abstains from flying the drone, or refuses to board the airplane that would take him to another country where the U.S. is engaged in illegal, immoral, unconscionable warfare.

---

48 See Overthrow by Stephan Kinzer. Details in bibliography.

NPR LIES

Once again I was listening to National People's Radio, NPR. I don't know if it's a case of boredom while driving, extreme annoyance of incessant commercials on other radio stations, or just a masochistic bent, but I keep doing it.[49]

On this particular day I heard a report on "All Things [Liberally] Considered" (ATC) on a bill in Congress which would add even more regulations to the financial industry. Now, I'm not one to defend the current state of the financial industry. They and the federal government have become one, mammoth mutual aid society. The cozy relationship between the national government and the banking industry has caused untold grief and disaster for individuals and society. But the slant of the report, the reporter, ATC, and NPR in general was as obvious as the pointed nose on my face. I didn't time the report, but I'd guess it was between three and four minutes in length. The first part was basically a diatribe about how only the government, with more regulations, could save the American people from the evil bankers and investment houses of Wall Street. Concerning the Republicans, the reporter actually stated that they were trying to "...block regulation of the financial industry." We heard much from the Democrat being interviewed about how the *evil Republicans* cared not a whit about the people's suffering and were controlled by their friends in the financial industry. To balance the report we heard a *one-sentence* response from a Republican—one solitary statement—that "the proposed bill would not help the American people." That was it. Period. End of story. The entire rebuttal was

---

49 Since writing this entry I have kicked the habit. I'm so proud of myself.

limited to exactly nine (9, count 'em, nine) words. There was no explanation of why those who voted against the bill did so. What was contained in the bill that they disagreed with? What is the alternate proposal? From NPR and All Things Liberally Considered we'll never know.

The making of a congressional bill, like sausage, is something those of sensitive constitutional makeup should never witness. Most bills in Congress are so long that our dear Congress-critters don't even read them. The length of the bill itself is multiplied at least by a factor of ten by the time an agency or commission, usually in the back pocket of industry insiders, writes the regulations that define it. Scratch that—it's normally the industry insiders themselves that not only write the bill, but the regulations that enforce it. As if that weren't enough, the bills are full of unrelated riders which are the negotiating chits among Congress-critters that push the bill through the process of buying enough votes to pass it.

And to say that the Republicans are trying to block regulation of the financial industry is beyond inaccurate; it is a bald-faced lie. The fact is that there are literally thousands of pages of regulations controlling every aspect of the financial industry; it is one of the most heavily regulated businesses in the country and the growth of regulation has not abated under any Republican regime.

To the extent that regulations allow abuse of consumers for the benefit of the power elite, that is the result of a completely bi-partisan effort to line the pockets of congress-critters and their corporate financial backers.

The NPR reporter knows this. The producers at NPR know this. The only reason they would allow such a one-sided report to be broadcast is because they are lap dogs of the government, and never more so than when there is a liberal regime in charge.

There's an old story that tells of a ship's first mate writing in the ship's log every few days, "The captain was not drunk today." After reaching port, the ship's owner read the log and fired the captain. In fact, the captain was sober every day of the voyage. Were the first mate's log entries lies? No. Did he lie in his log entries? Yes. There is a reason witnesses in court proceedings swear to tell not just the truth, but the *whole* truth. Anything less is a lie.

I'm no fan of Republicans, but neither am I a fan of lying. NPR has become the master of selective truth-telling to support all things liberal and to do everything in their power to get the conservative captain fired.

HAVE YOU NO SHAME, SENATOR?

I read that Afghanistan received money from Iran, and the United States is all atwitter about it. Seems to me like the pot calling the kettle black—in spades. (Not to belabor the black thing.) Apparently the *New York Times* reported that Iranian officials once gave the Afghanistan president's chief of staff a bag stuffed with American currency as "*part of a secret, steady stream of Iranian cash.*" The state Department says it doesn't question the right of Iran to give money to Afghanistan, nor does it question the right of Afghanistan to receive it. But they said, "We remain skeptical of Iran's motives, given its history of playing a *destabilizing* role with its neighbors. A White House spokesman, Bill Burton, had these further words, "I think the American people and the global community have every reason to believe that—or every reason to be concerned about Iran trying to have a negative influence on Afghanistan."

Excuse me for wondering what gives the American government the *cajones* to even make a statement concerning from whom Afghanistan receives money, much less make a statement to the effect that they feel the American people have every reason to be concerned about anyone trying to have a *negative* influence on any country.

Did the American government not have a destabilizing, negative influence on Hawaii after Navy and Marine troops took over that island nation in the nineteenth century? Did the Americans not have a destabilizing influence in Nicaragua, Guatemala, and El Salvador all through the twentieth century? Did the Americans not have a destabilizing influence at various times in the histories of Argentina, Chile, Viet Nam, Cambodia, Laos, North and South Korea, Pakistan, Iraq, Cuba, The

Philippines, various African countries, and more that only the president and the CIA know about? And some that only the CIA know of?

Can there be any greater display of *chutzpah* than the United States saying *anything* at all about Iran giving cash to Afghanistan? If the government of the U.S. had any remaining ability to show any amount of shame, this would be the time.

Unfortunately, the sentiment of shame is something the United States government has long since given up.

LOVE OF COUNTRY

I love my children, I love my parents, and as one of God's children, I do my best to love you.

But I do not love my country.

That statement has nothing to do with the fact that I believe the government, under which I am forced to live, to be well on the way to creating an evil, world-encompassing empire out of the once-great ideals of Jefferson, Adams, Paine, et al.

My sentiments have nothing to do with the government's usurpation of power well beyond that granted by the Constitution.

Neither do my sentiments have anything to do with the problems of American society, or the military/industrial/governmental complex (the Deep State) that has come to control the daily lives of every citizen of the U.S., and exerts some amount of influence on every inhabitant of the Earth.

The reason I don't love my country is simply that I don't understand how it is necessary, proper, desirable, or even possible to love a political creation.

I have read the New Testament several times and have studied it in depth. I don't find anywhere in it a suggestion that I should love my country. I don't believe that everything of importance in life is spelled out in the Bible, but if I could find a reference to love of country in it I would at least give it serious consideration. Neither have I been able to figure out why it is that I should love the country in which I was born, simply because it is the place of my birth, placing it in importance over and above the people, lands, and cultures of the rest of the world.

One might respond that loving your country does not imply that you hold it above all other peoples, lands, and cultures, but if this is not the end result and outward manifestation of love of country, then what is the purpose? If there is no outward manifestation of the emotion, then why is it seen as so important to feel it?

I love my children because they are my children; they are part of me. I was given the responsibility to care for them in a spiritual and physical sense. Should they be in danger or need my help, I respond to that need because I love them, and only because I love them. My love for them is unconditional; bad or good, they are my children and I would give my life for them if required. I place them above my own personal interests, not because they deserve it (although, gratefully, they do), but because I love them. There is a spiritual, emotional, and physical bond of love between them and me because they are my children. That bond will never be broken, even by death.

I love my brothers and sister and parents in the same way. If I were perfect, I would genuinely love every person in the world. I am far from that ideal, but I still aspire to it. My belief is that the very purpose of Jesus' life on this Earth was to demonstrate the true nature of perfect love, the true nature of God, and to say that we should, imperfect as we are, at least try to act as though we love every other human on Earth as God himself loves us.

But the word "love," when applied to one's country cannot possibly have the same meaning. My country right or wrong, good or evil? Does love of country mean I should give my life for it, as I would for my children, my brothers, my sister, and my parents? Millions would say yes. But where is the spiritual bond between my country and me? Did God entrust me with the care and nurturing of my country, a political entity by definition and in practice, so that I should place it above all other peoples and cultures? If I do so, how am I to sincerely pursue the perfect love of other people, no matter within which political borders they reside? Is the moral discontinuity not apparent to everyone?

I cannot understand how loving my culture or the land and people within the borders of the territory known as the United States of America can possibly exist concurrently with the love of all people, regardless of where they were born. The whole concept makes no sense to me.

I can understand loyalty, and even a deep, emotional feeling toward those of your family, clan, or small nation (as in the Hopi Nation, for example) and the desire to protect them, but love for an expanse of land and a mix of cultures as large and varied as the United States is incomprehensible.

I am psychically comfortable with my culture because I have been raised in it, and I truly wish it could be preserved, but that is not to say that it is somehow more worthy of my love than other cultures. The arts are a vital component of the culture, but the arts in the United States are the extension of a long lineage of arts from other countries and cultures. The varied foods come from every culture of the world. I enjoy Mexican, Japanese, Cantonese, Mediterranean, Brazilian, Philippine, and just about every other type and style of food I've tasted (if I might be allowed to ignore poi).

No, I still can't find the thing I'm supposed to love about my country over and above other countries and peoples of the world.

One might say, "You should love your country because in America you have the opportunity to be free, to pursue your dreams, to enjoy other cultures, earn enough money to enjoy the arts and food from all parts of the world. For heaven's sake, look at how bad it is in other countries!"

The same rationale could be used in answer to a complaining slave two hundred years ago. "Look how good you have it on my plantation! The masters in other plantations beat their slaves much more than I, and you get Saturday afternoon and all day Sunday off. The other plantation owners make their slaves work all day Saturday. You ought to love me!"

The fact that we are supposedly allowed to enjoy a little more of our God-given freedom here than elsewhere, and that there is a little more respect for property rights and the rule of law here than in some other countries is no consolation. (Thousands of new laws and regulations over the past several years have eviscerated even that argument.)

According to the founders of this nation, prior to the forming of any government we already had and continue to have *all* basic human rights because they were granted to us by our Creator. We only delegate certain responsibilities, and limit a few of our natural rights to maintain peace and order in society. If the government abides by the contract agreed to by my forebears over two centuries ago, that is no more reason to love this country than to love my landlord because he obeys the agreement set forth in the lease we both agreed to.

In fact, I would argue from the opposite direction. I have never agreed to any contract between the government and myself. Whether I agree with any law or regulation under which I am forced to live has no bearing on the fact that I am still *forced* to live with it. The very fact that I am only allowed to enjoy whatever freedom the government allows is not freedom in any sense of the word.

The borders of this country we are supposed to love were drawn in blood. The government took what it wanted through war and subjugation and doled it out to those whom it chose. The current rulers, from the lineage of those original rulers, want and expect me to feel love for my country so that they can use that emotion to their benefit. If I love my country I will fight and die for it, right or wrong. I will be patriotic and defend my land (my government) against all enemies. (They will do everything in their power to obfuscate the fact that those enemies are defined and primarily created by the State.) If I love my country I will obey my rulers in times of emergency, even though those very same rulers have <u>caused</u> the emergency.

Love of country is an idea that our rulers need us to embrace in order to pursue *their* goals. If you love your country, right or wrong, you'll give your life, or worse, the lives of your children for the next war our rulers choose to wage. If you love your country, you may complain about the high taxes and the corrupt government and the daily loss of liberty but ultimately you'll put red, white, and blue bumper stickers and yellow ribbon magnets on your car and fly the U.S. battle flag in front of your house and wave it at Independence Day parades. You'll say, "I don't agree with everything my government does, but I love my country and I'm sure glad I wasn't born in Whateveritstan."

So when we invade and bomb Whateveritstan for their oil or their strategic location on the planet, or just to teach 'em who's boss, we'll all be able to sit back, wrapped in our American battle flag, and we'll sleep well at night, feeling safe, secure, and morally superior in our love of country.

Patriotism

That last chapter, I'm sure, rubbed a lot of my conservative readers the wrong way; we are, all of us, inculcated with a strong sense of patriotism from our earliest days and regardless of political persuasion, we still instinctively want to be part of, and have pride in, a group. Inexplicably, that group, at its largest manifestation, tends to be the State that controls the borders of the region of the Earth in which one is born and lives. (That State today is referenced by the word country—love of the *state of the union* in which one was born and lived was pretty well dealt the death blow, sadly, in 1865.)

This is not so in every region of the Earth. Many Catalunyans tend to identify more strongly with Catalunya, and most Basques identify more strongly with The Basque Country than with Spain. I admit I don't have knowledge of every region of the world, but I can only assume there are other instances where regional patriotism is stronger than national. You'll find this in any region of the world where people of diverse cultures are forced to live under one political regime. But here in The United States, national pride is taken as a given, and those who don't feel and display sufficient patriotism are treated as social outcasts and traitors, as unworthy, low-life scum.

I can understand the sentiments of those who feel showing patriotic spirit is the highest calling of all Americans. I've heard the arguments:

> America has given you so much.
> Men have died so that you can be free.
> This is the best nation on Earth.
> America is exceptional.
> America is God's shining beacon on a hill, an example to the poor and downtrodden around the globe.

And all those points may be true (or not), but are they not by any rational standard subjective? The point of this essay is not to argue whether the United States deserves to be revered, but to say that, one, all the reasons one might give for that reverence are, in fact, purely subjective, and two, nobody has the right, especially in the "freest country on Earth" to force others to conform to his opinion, even opinions regarding the religion of patriotism.

You may believe the city in which you live is the best city in the country, and that this is the best country on the face of the planet, and therefore everyone should sing (literally) your city's praises and stand at attention to its flag as the greatest city on Earth. Perhaps the neighborhoods are kept clean by the city sanitation workers, the dogs are all friendly, the women are beautiful, and all the children are above average. Would it not make sense to harangue any citizens of your city who did not agree with you concerning the standing of your city vis-à-vis all others in the world and did not rise to attention before your city's flag? But nobody does this. Why not?

Maybe your county has the best fair. Maybe the cows are fatter, the corn is more plentiful, and the water is sweeter than in any other county in the country. And since your county exists in the best country in the world, it then logically follows that yours is the best county in the world. Therefore citizens of the county who don't sing your county anthem and hold a right hand over his heart is an ungrateful SOB. But nobody feels this way. Why not?

Prior to the War for Southern Independence people were loyal to and died for their state. Remember, it was thirteen *independent states (countries),* each of whom considered themselves politically equal with any of the *states (countries)* of Europe, such as France, Spain, and Switzerland, that signed the peace treaty with Great

Britain. After that war and the defeat of the Confederate States of America, "The United States" morphed from a plural to a singular noun, and all citizens of the United States of America were required to declare their loyalty to the national government, an abomination the founding fathers would never have approved of. The populace ever since has been taught that their greatest loyalty belongs to the National Government. If you accept this, that is your prerogative, but by what moral authority do you require this of everyone else?

Certainly one of the founding principles of this nation was that of the right of free expression. The words of Voltaire were familiar to all of the founding fathers: "Think for yourselves and let others enjoy the privilege to do so also." (From his *Essay on Tolerance*.) And do we not firmly believe, "I disapprove of what you say, but I will defend to the death your right to say it"? (Evelyn Beatrice Hall, writing as S. G. Tallentyre.) We seem to hold to those beliefs until the matter comes to the appropriate public demonstration of patriotism toward the United States of America.

Do we not also cherish the right to protest? To speak our mind? Is freedom of expression not a cornerstone of our republic? It seems that most of us believe this until such expression takes the form of not standing tall before what is, in truth, the *battle flag* of the early republic and displaying reverence for one of the few national hymns of any country in the world that actually celebrates warfare. We seem to demand others' protests with which we disagree be carried out in a manner that suits us and that is not apparent to too many people. We say, "If you want to protest what you feel is the unfair treatment of black people by the police, then by all means write a letter to the editor that few will read. Parade up and down in front of a police station where few will see you. But do not deign to demonstrate your feelings where millions of people may observe, especially if you are going to dishonor the battle flag during the national hymn of warfare!"

Your loyalty to a government is your business. Your display of such loyalty is your business. Others born and living within the borders controlled by the government of the United States my feel differently, and until we make the next great turning, the right to express that feeling or opinion is still a sacred right and you have absolutely no moral authority to deny it.

The bottom line is, in the United States of America, as founded and as currently exists, no one has the obligation to display fealty to the national government nor to its symbols. Denying differences of opinion and demonstrations of those opinions is inimical to the founding principles of this nation. This is the case even if those opinions and demonstrations run counter to the principles of the nation itself.

HAVE WE HAD ENOUGH YET?

What's it going to take? We have "free speech zones," limiting the unfettered political free speech that was the intent of the founders of this country. We have government meddling in religion in direct contradiction of the founder's principles. The federal government has, without a doubt, abridged our right to keep and bear arms. Warrantless wiretapping, legalized torture, indefinite detention, military involvement in domestic police operations... The list goes on and on.

And now we have to undergo electronic strip searches in order to fly on an airplane. Of course you don't have to go through the porno-scanners; you can "opt out" and instead receive an "enhanced pat down" which, if performed by anyone other than a blue-shirt government goon would land that person in jail with a life-long record of a sex predator.

To prove the point that people will put up with absolutely anything if you just give them time to become accustomed to it, most Americans seem to be perfectly comfortable with not only an electronic strip search, but the gross loss of human rights at the hands of the federal government over the last several decades. There's always a "good reason" for the loss of our rights—the drug war, the war on terrorism, protecting us from militant foreigners, protecting us from our neighbors, protecting us from ourselves—in general, protecting us from the vicissitudes of liberty. A talented politician (I originally wrote "good politician," but that's an oxymoron) can always come up with a reason to do anything, especially when they only have to convince Boobus Americanus, beneficiary of the American education (sic) system.

We are sheep being led to the slaughter and too few people care. The United States of America is rapidly becoming a failed experiment in a free people governing themselves. Are we going to be willing accomplices to our own enslavement? There is a small but rapidly growing resistance to this latest encroachment on our human rights. Join the fight. Refuse to fly on any airline unless and until those companies start standing up to the *federales*. They are not our betters. We are not their slaves. The airlines can stand to lose business from a few thousand; they cannot stand the loss of business of a few million. Write letters to the airlines and tell them that you will not be using their services as long as TSA goons man their *Checkpoint Charlies* and treat us as conquered subjects.

I am an enemy of the State.

In "Rightwing Extremism: Current Economic and Political Climate Fueling Resurgence in Radicalization and Recruitment"[50] you'll find the following definition:

> *Rightwing extremism in the United States can be broadly divided into those groups, movements, and adherents that ... are mainly antigovernment, rejecting federal authority in favor of state or local authority, or rejecting government authority entirely."* It continues with *"Historically, domestic rightwing extremists have feared, predicted, and anticipated a cataclysmic economic collapse in the United States. Conspiracy theories involving declarations of martial law, impending civil strife or racial conflict, suspension of the U.S. Constitution, and the creation of citizen detention camps often incorporate aspects of a failed economy. Antigovernment conspiracy theories and "end times" prophecies could motivate extremist individuals and groups to stockpile food, ammunition, and weapons.*

I've got news for the authors of this report at the Department of Homeland (better said, *Der Heimatland*) Security. It's not only rightwing extremists who hold these opinions. Those of us who are neither right nor left, but value the original principles of liberty that this country was founded upon find ourselves squarely implanted in this definition.

Government is that entity that uses force or the threat of force to coerce people within geographic boundaries to do

---

50 (http://www.fas.org/irp/eprint/rightwing.pdf)

what it wants them to do, or to not do what it does not want them to do. As a libertarian and an anarchist, I am against using force and the threat of violence to force people to live according to my wishes, and I would certainly appreciate others treating me in the same manner. It is unfortunate that in the world in which we live, there is no physical space remaining that is not under the control of a State government that will force those who are born or immigrate within its boundaries to live according to its wishes, including most importantly, the claim of a part of every ounce of productivity that might emanate from that person (income taxation).

If I have to live under the power of a group of people who hold a monopoly on the use of force, then I favor the devolution of government to its smallest possible application. If this is extremism, then I'm as extreme as Thomas Jefferson and a host of other founders who designed the federal government. Check your dictionary—federal is not a synonym for national. The founders did not create an overpowering *national* government, but a federation of independent states that constituted a voluntarily agreement among otherwise independent states for the purpose of protecting them against invasion from without, for the purpose of arbitration of disagreements among them, and for guaranteeing free trade within the union. If I am forced to live under the power of government, then yes, I wholly reject national government authority in preference of state and local authority. Better to keep the devil close at hand.

Even if I voluntarily supported the murderous, conniving, imperialistic nature of the U.S. national government, I would still be an extremist because I can see no end to the government of this country other than a declaration of martial law because of the coming economic collapse caused by its short-sighted economic policies—enabled by the Federal Reserve Bank—and the U.S. foreign (war) policy of constant stirring of hornets' nests around the globe. For all practical purposes, the Constitution has already been suspended; the Bill of Rights is completely ignored by the executive and legislative branches, and they are enabled by the judicial branch.

Yes, I admit, I am one of those extremists but not right or left wing, thank you. I am simply a lover of liberty who understands that the very nature and fundamental principles of the State are immoral. For that reason, and for that reason alone, I count myself among the thousands upon thousands of proud Enemies of the State.

HITLER DIDN'T KILL ANYONE

"Poor, wretched, and stupid peoples, nations determined on your own misfortune and blind to your own good! You let yourselves be deprived before your own eyes of the best part of your revenues; your fields are plundered, your homes robbed, your family heirlooms taken away. You live in such a way that you cannot claim a single thing as your own; and it would seem that you consider yourselves lucky to be loaned your property, your families, and your very lives. All this havoc, this misfortune, this ruin, descends upon you not from alien foes, but from the one enemy whom you yourselves render as powerful as he is, for whom you go bravely to war, for whose greatness you do not refuse to offer your own bodies unto death. He who thus domineers over you has only two eyes, only two hands, only one body, no more than is possessed by the least man among the infinite numbers dwelling in your cities; he has indeed nothing more than the power that you confer upon him to destroy you.

"Where has he acquired enough eyes to spy upon you, if you do not provide them yourselves? How can he have so many arms to beat you with, if he does not borrow them from you? The feet that trample down your cities, where does he get them if they are not your own? How does he have any power over you except through you? How would he dare assail you if he had no cooperation from you? What could he do to you if you yourselves did not connive with the thief who plunders you, if you were not accomplices of the murderer who kills you, if you were not traitors to yourselves? You sow your crops in order that he may ravage them, you install and furnish your homes to give him goods to pillage; you rear your daughters that he may gratify his lust; you bring up your children in

order that he may confer upon them the greatest privilege he knows—to be led into his battles, to be delivered to butchery, to be made the servants of his greed and the instruments of his vengeance; you yield your bodies unto hard labor in order that he may indulge in his delights and wallow in his filthy pleasures; you weaken yourselves in order to make him the stronger and the mightier to hold you in check. From all these indignities, such as the very beasts of the field would not endure, you can deliver yourselves if you try, not by taking action, but merely by willing to be free.

"Resolve to serve no more, and you are at once freed. I do not ask that you place hands upon the tyrant to topple him over, but simply that you support him no longer; then you will behold him, like a great Colossus whose pedestal has been pulled away, fall of his own weight and break into pieces."

Étienne de la Boétie

Somewhere, deep in the historical archives of German army history there may be a record of Adolph Hitler having killed someone during his service, rising to the vaulted rank of corporal in the First World War. But I've never heard of it, never read it, have never seen any mention of *Herr Hitler* pulling the trigger to kill a single human.

What I have read of, and have no doubt of, is that he ordered other people to kill or do things that resulted in the deaths of millions of people.

But what does that say about the millions of people who dutifully followed orders or stood by while others followed his orders, or those of his political and military accomplices to pursue courses of action that, by any standard of human decency were barbaric and atrocious and define the boundaries of pure evil? What does this say about those who were ultimately responsible, those who performed the millions of acts of cruelty? What are we to make of the millions of individuals who blindly followed the call to arms, followed the drums to war, and physically performed the billions of barbarous actions on individual humans for which Herr Hitler is blamed? At the moment of death at the hands of one person, there is no collective guilt. There is no society, no group-think, no social order, nor obeisance to superiors. There is only one simple reality—one human by his own volition killing another. The will to take that action may have been the result of a long sequence of previous decisions and actions that make the ultimate act of killing one, hundreds, or thousands of humans very difficult, if not virtually impossible to avoid without risk to the perpetrator's own life. Nonetheless, that death and destruction of life and property is the result of personal, individual decisions.

Lest someone think that I am singling out people within early twentieth century Germany for special treatment, there were much more egregious and numerous acts of inhumanity in the Soviet Union, in China not only during Mao's revolution but in numerous periods through her history, in Cambodia, and, yes, even in the United States in the nineteenth century as we, either with government sanction or at the hand of government forces themselves, wiped out entire nations of Native Americans, and the people of the states that comprised the Confederate States of America.

Even the most evil men cannot hold a candle to the combined evil of thousands or millions of subservients who willingly perform acts of evil in their leaders' names. There is no force that makes them do these things other than their *own will* to take part in the evil. For Hitler to have been stopped, or for that matter Pol Pot, Mao, Sherman, Lincoln, Stalin, Johnson, Nixon, Bush, Obama, or any other mass murderers in history, all that would have been required is for each individual at the killing end of the arrangement to say "No, I am not going to do evil. I am not going to kill for you. I refuse to sacrifice my humanity."

INSURGENT MATH

In Afghanistan for every insurgent killed, ten more insurgents are created by the collateral damage to (murder of) civilians. Every coalition attack leads to six retaliatory attacks against our troops within the following six weeks. This doesn't surprise anyone. It doesn't surprise Gen. McChrystal or his replacement, Gen. Petraeus, or the Joint Chiefs of Staff or the president of the U.S. himself, Mr. Obama. They all know that every action by American troops in a foreign country results in violent actions against Americans, which then have to be retaliated against, which are then avenged, which then have to be retaliated against, *ad infinitum*. (Hatfields and McCoys?) You might think that at some point someone could wake up and realize that our actions in foreign countries are promoting the very thing we claim to be fighting: terrorism.

This is where we need to step back and look at the situation from a different perspective. If such bright people keep doing the same "irrational" things, maybe it is we who are missing the point. It should be obvious by now that our rulers and the military, congressional, and industrial fellow travelers are not interested in the security and safety of the "American people." No, they are interested in the security and safety of the American Welfare/Warfare State Apparatus (the National Government) and the ruling elite, the One Tenth of One Percent, the Oligarchs who pull all the strings. They are concerned with themselves and only themselves. As Randolph Bourne said, "War is the health of the State." Rulers and politicians have always encouraged wars in order to advance the power of the State. That the rulers of the U.S. would do the same, aided and abetted by the military, congressional, and industrial interests (The Deep State) who share in the lucre, should surprise only those who still cling to the idea that Obama and his ilk, or any part of the U.S. government, are sincere in what they state as their motives for every policy they promote.

Every organism has as its prime motivation its continued existence and growth. The American government is the largest organism on the planet. But the organism is a cancer. Unfortunately, it has grown too large to contain and it will continue to grow until it destroys its host.

It's unfortunate that millions of innocents have to go down with it.

Here's a hypothetical for you: How much tax would the government collect from General Motors and its dealers tomorrow for the day's business if not one person showed up for work? No one to assemble cars. No one to sell cars. No one to manage financing. No one to repair cars. No one to maintain the computers that control manufacturing, dealer communication, and personnel records. No one to program computers, to design cars and systems, to answer phones. What if everyone from the president and CEO to the guy who cleans the bathrooms just stayed home from work? How much money would GM earn and how much would the government collect in tax from the company for that day?

Easy answer: $0.00.

That's because a public corporation, LLC, sole proprietorship, or whatever legal form a business enterprise takes pays no tax. None. It's not a difficult concept, but it's one that completely escapes the vast majority of people.

Revenue that flows to a business of any kind goes to one of very few broad but easily definable categories. Business income that is not paid to employees and owners flows to plant and equipment, research and development, or retained earnings. Taxes that the government takes from that business come from one of those pools.

Funds that maintain and grow plant and equipment provide a safe and effective work place to humans and enable the efficient manufacture of goods and creation of services the company offers to the market. To the extent that plant and equipment is maintained and is modern and efficient, it helps the enterprise to continue earning profits and paying its employees and owners—who pay income taxes.

Research and development allows the business to maintain its competitive position within its market and allows the business to grow with new and better products and services. To the extent that R&D is effective and creates new and better products and services, it allows the enterprise to continue earning profits and paying its employees and owners—who pay income taxes.

Retained earnings is the business's savings account that enables it to weather business downturns or finance future growth without having to borrow or dilute ownership by selling additional shares of the company. An appropriate level of retained earnings protects the business from an uncertain future and to take advantage of opportunities quickly, possibly allowing it to gain advantageous market position faster than competitors, thus giving the enterprise a better chance of staying in business. If retained earnings are inadequate, the company faces more risk than it ideally should. The company may find itself unable to weather a business downturn or take advantage of changing market conditions. If the balance of the retained earnings account is too high, the owners (shareholders) will rightfully say that those funds are not being used to the best advantage for the enterprise and will (or should) force management to make better use of scarce financial resources for the good of the company. In either case, a judicious balance in retained earnings and its wise use benefits the enterprise and helps it to stay in business, paying salaries to employees and paying a fair return to owners—who pay income taxes.

Note that in all cases, plant and equipment, research and development, and retained earnings, properly managed, are components of a well-run, sustainable business that earns and pays salaries and dividends to employees and owners, those *human beings* that actually perform the creative activity of the business and are the *only* source of income that the government can tax.

If the government taxes the revenue of the business, those funds are not available to it to perform its operations that create revenue and, so, must reduce the business's ability to operate, grow, and ultimately provide income and dividends to employees and owners. Taxing revenue of the enterprise before it reaches the individual human beings who actually produce it is no different from an income withholding tax; it is an onerous method of hiding the fact that the government is taking more money from individuals than they realize. The government is benefiting from the fact that the vast majority of people do not recognize that business entities themselves do not actually pay taxes, but that the tax revenue is taken out of the system from its true owners before they even see the money. That the governments of the world get away with this is testament to the business ignorance of the general population and more, a testament to envy. Most people like nothing more than to see businesses pay "their fair share." Never mind that "fair share" cannot be defined and that those tax revenues are only diverted from the source before they reach their rightful destinations—those employees and owners, the humans, who are actually the creators and rightful direct and indirect beneficiaries of all business revenue. By taking the money before it reaches its rightful recipient, the government is able to disguise how much it is actually taking from its citizens.

Only humans pay taxes.

Surprise! Your Beliefs May Not Be My Beliefs

You may firmly believe that crossing yourself and kneeling when you walk before an altar, above which hangs a cross holding a representation of Christ Jesus, is an absolute requirement. If that is your faith, and if that is an expectation of your faith, then you should, by all means, perform the ritual.

If you firmly believe that there is no God but Allah and that Mohammed is his prophet, then you will be required to pray facing Mecca five times per day. You will also expect others who so believe to do likewise. (You may believe that everyone on Earth should also believe the same or die, but we'll ignore that; I'm only writing for civilized, rational people.)

In both cases, the believer has every moral right to expect other *believers* to observe the same honorific actions. It's part of the faith, and part of the unspoken agreement between faith and believer.

It is the case that there are rituals of faith that are followed by its members. Of that there is no question. Those who *voluntarily*, of sound, adult mind join or maintain membership in a faith group knowing the ritual expectations, should be expected by other members of the group to practice those rituals. Members of such a faith group have a right to expect fellow members to comport themselves in a manner in agreement with the group's norms, customs, and values.

But if I am not of that faith, then you have no moral right or any other basis to demand that I accede to your expectations or perform rituals of your faith. We in the traditionally liberal (old-fashioned usage, which root is the same as the word "liberty") western world normally agree with that stance; such a show of faith and respect is expected of those *who are of that faith*. Those who believe otherwise are not normally castigated and reviled. A non-Catholic, for example, is not criticized for not genuflecting before a representation of Jesus in a church.

But concerning my residence within the borders of any country, where and when did I voluntarily join an organization that requires that I stand before your sacred cloth symbol and sing your sacred song? Whence comes your moral authority to demand that I behave according to your sense of propriety simply based on an accident of birth? What is your logical, rational, and moral argument for forcing me to think as you think, feel as you feel, and act as you act?

Our American society tells us we should allow others to observe other's beliefs and act in accordance therewith. That is part of our American culture we can justly be proud of. They are not obligated in any way to observe our rituals or act in accord with our beliefs, as long as those beliefs concern religion, sexual behavior, rites of passage, or anything other than our nationality. But when one of the faith of TrueBlueAmerican observes someone who happened to have been born within the borders under control of the government of the United States of America who does not recite the Pledge of Allegiance and sing the national hymn and show the proper obeisance to the government military forces, and demonstrate all that with verve and feeling(!), then the gloves come off. TrueBlueAmericans consider such a non-action a slap in the face not only to themselves but especially to everyone who has ever worn a uniform or carried a gun at the behest of the U.S. government. In such a case, there is no respect for different opinions or beliefs. That infidel is to be shunned and verbally castigated, figuratively if not literally thrown out of polite, TrueBlueAmerican society. There is no longer any respect for personal beliefs or personal feelings. For some inexplicable reason, the limit of tolerance finds its end at the demonstration of Nationalism and Patriotic Pride. From that there is no allowable deviation.

This is especially so at Grand, National Sporting Events that have become hours-long commercial spots for U.S. military forces. That these same public displays of reverence are an absolute requirement by totalitarian governments of the Earth should give any rational person pause to consider whether that same action falls within the realm of the obligations of a free people. Yet millions upon millions of TrueBlueAmericans cannot consider for a second that one's display of such fealty is purely a personal matter and of no concern to anyone else, or that a demonstration of fealty to an increasingly over-bearing government *just might not* be a good thing.

Would you consider it a slap in your face if I did not genuflect before the representation of your god or pray five times toward your holy city? Of course not. (Again, I'm writing for civilized, rational people.) Then why are you so insulted if I do not rise in front of the symbol of a political region or sing its hymn?

Is the United States of America the land of the free or is it not?

Your personal beliefs and displays of fealty are your business. That another does not share your beliefs and does not demonstrate those non-feelings to suit you, even when given a national spotlight, is not your concern. The United States of America is not a religion.

RUSSIAN SCIENCE?

Loren Graham asks why Russian science, if it's so amazing, hasn't taken over the world?"[51] The first and most obvious answer to his question is that there is no such thing as *Russian science.*

Mr. Graham has fallen victim to the mindset that is in fact inhibiting the scientific discoveries and developments made by people within that country from becoming commercially viable: *Countries* do not invent or create anything. A country is a political hoax; it is a creation of a relatively small group of people who want to control others. Unfortunately, what they typically want to control is the creative energy and output of the people within their sphere of influence for the purpose of collecting tribute, otherwise known as taxes. To the extent that they allow the free flow of ideas and technology, the people benefit. Those whose vision of reality is seen from the perspective of social and political groups then attribute success to a country. We do this with science as we do with sport. Look up Olympic medal winners on Wikipedia and every person who has won a medal is associated with their country. Golfers in championship tournaments are always identified with their country. Yet, the country did not put in the years of practice and discipline that resulted in an Olympic medal or the bright green jacket—the individual, and only the individual did. Countries are not imbued with raw athletic talent or mental abilities. As with science and any form of creativity, intelligence, entrepreneurship, and hard work are the purview of individuals. The best that a government can do is get out of the way and allow

---

51 https://www.bostonglobe.com/ideas/2015/01/04/russian-science-amazing-why-hasn-taken-over-world/u61VuLiq3lJiyIMY0OLZ7N/story.html

individuals to succeed. Government has one and only one role in any individual's success: protect his or her right to pursue personal goals and the right to benefit from any advances their mental and physical prowess may provide to other individuals.

Loren Graham has spent years trying to understand how Russia, given its number of people who have made great scientific discoveries, could be such a backwater in technology. I think he's missing the forest for the trees. The government of Russia simply has not allowed individuals to sufficiently profit from their work. A Russian application programmer may imagine the next great "killer app," but if there is no possibility of profiting from it there is no incentive to dedicate himself to the years of hard work, to say nothing of the financial risk of commercializing an invention. This is something that great "intellectuals" seem to miss time and time again: Entrepreneurs, as politicians, act in their self-interest. The difference is, while entrepreneurs benefit themselves by offering the public something that may improve their lives in *voluntary* exchange for money, politicians benefit themselves by *forcing* others to act or not act, to buy or not buy. They make back room deals that accrue profits to themselves and their cronies at the expense of those who have actually created something of value to others.

Fortunately, in the United States and some other countries there is still the possibility that an individual can benefit from his or her creativity, intelligence, and entrepreneurship. In the old Soviet Union and in today's Russia, that is much less the case. To the extent that there is any capitalism in Russia today it seems to be, for the most part, pure crony capitalism, which is not capitalism at all. So if a person within the borders of Russia has the ability and will to develop new technology, but the political class cannot see a way to profit from it, it dies on the vine or the idea somehow gets passed to someone within a political hegemon that still allows individual profit. It's accepted that the individual who profits is probably not the one who deserves it, and so those who deserve the benefit are less likely to put in the creative energy in the first place. If there is no incentive to plant a seed, then no seed will be planted and nothing will grow.

The answer to Loren Graham's question is simple: The people within the confines of the Russian borders could develop and benefit from technology, and export that technology for the benefit of people around the world, if only the government would get the hell out of the way.

LIBERALS AND CONSERVATIVES

Recently I've noticed a rash of Facebook posts along the lines of, "It's official. Republicans are stupid," or "It's an indisputable fact: Republicans want to starve children and poison the world," or "The reason Republicans don't like Mr. Obama is because they're just not intelligent enough to understand him."

I have no doubt that there are similar posts directed at Democrats, but they don't seem to cross my Facebook page for some reason. That's not to say I don't receive posts concerning Mr. Obama's desire to rule as a dictator by executive order, ignore the Constitution, and turn the United States into something more befitting the northern European socialist model.

As an aside, I personally I don't find those comments about the president at all untrue. I don't see any Democrat or liberal posts that deny they'd prefer to model a new U.S. constitution after Norway, Denmark, or Sweden, and the pattern for almost every president since the founding of the country has been to increase power at every opportunity, and to actively create those opportunities whenever possible.

Getting back to the point, there seems to be a lack of civility between the liberal and conservative camps, if I may wildly understate the phenomenon. This is nothing new; the two major parties controlling the United States government have a long history of uncivil behavior, including but not limited to fist fights on the floor of the House of Representatives, members of Congress beating each other with canes, and duels with pistols at dawn.

But isn't it time to move past all that and discuss issues rationally in an adult, intelligent manner?

Voltaire said, "If you wish to converse with me, first define your terms." He meant more than just the words you use; he meant there can be no meaningful discussion if we don't understand, and not just understand but acknowledge, the fundamental, underlying philosophy of the other party. Politicians don't want to do that because their reason for existence is power and the money that flows from it. The path of least resistance in their case is to paint their opponent as not intelligent enough to do the job or to convince his supporters that the opponent is simply evil, someone who should be banished to a desert island for the safety of the public. If they succeed in convincing their constituency of their opponent's unworthiness for whatever reason, they win as, if nothing else, the lesser of two evils. Winning ugly is still winning. And winning is the whole point of politics.

But do we have to play their game?

There's one major philosophy that says many ideas and behaviors of the past worked well to ensure an orderly, peaceful society where people who so desired could succeed financially, or in whatever other definition of success suited them. All was not perfect, but change came slowly through careful and thoughtful adjustment of ideas, voluntarily, one person at a time. Customs and values of the past were highly valued and not thrown overboard lightly. Thomas Jefferson said it best when he wrote "Prudence, indeed, will dictate that Governments long established should not be changed for light and transient causes; and accordingly all experience hath shown, that mankind are more disposed to suffer, while evils are sufferable, than to right themselves by abolishing the forms to which they are accustomed." Just substitute "traditions and customs" for "government." Those who would conserve institutions that served well in the past are conservatives, and they mostly populate the Republican Party. These people also tend to view the world from the perspective of the individual, from the "atomic" level. The individual has liberty, has abilities, and is responsible for himself. Those few who cannot, for whatever reason, take care of themselves are best served by *voluntary* charity, beginning with their own families, which conservatives see as, and in truth has been throughout human history, the basic social unit.

There's another philosophy that looks at the world from the top down—the overall society is the core, fundamental object of concern. These people are liberals or progressives (by current definition), and they, for the most part, populate the Democrat Party. Even though they envision a classless society, they acknowledge that there is a class of people who are more intelligent than most others, and these people are able to design societal institutions that will direct individuals, as a society, to better ways of living, more humane and just ways of interacting with each other, and more efficient ways of providing for the least among us.

The people who view society from the top down are not evil and they're certainly not unintelligent. There is ample evidence of suffering, by individuals and entire groups, and of misdirected efforts of large groups of people against others to fortify their opinions of how best to formulate public policy.

Those who view the world from the perspective of the individual and have the dynamic history of the United States as evidence of what individual ingenuity can do, the great strides that can be taken in an environment of individual liberty when it's allowed to flourish, are not evil and certainly are not unintelligent.

The basic problem is that both sides have a common desire: that a massive, all powerful government control the daily lives of hundreds of millions of individuals. Those same hundreds of millions who make up the groups called liberals and conservatives do not necessarily want to control their fellow citizens, but the leaders of those groups certainly do, and they are the ones who get elected and appointed to government offices. We humans seem to have a gene in our DNA that is either on or off—we either want to be a leader or a follower. And those who want to follow will go to any lengths, give up anything, even their birthright and will ignore their moral compasses to have and follow a strong leader. This has always been so.

First Samuel, Chapter 8, verses 1 through 20. Tradition says this was written around 600 BC.

> *When Samuel was old he appointed his sons judges over Israel. Samuel's first son was named Joel, has second, Abijah; they were judges in Beersheba. His sons, however, did not walk in his ways, but turned aside and followed the path of graft and corruption; they accepted bribes and perverted justice. Then all the elders of Israel gathered together and came to Samuel at Ramah; They said to him. "Look, you have grown old and your sons do not follow your example. Now appoint for us a king to judge us like all the other nations. But when they said, "Give us a king to judge us," this displeased Samuel. So he prayed to the Lord. And the Lord responded to Samuel's prayer, "Listen to all that the people have said to you. They have not rejected you, but they have rejected Me as King over them. Just as everything they did since the day I brought them out of Egypt, and even to this day—in that they have forsaken Me and served other gods—so they are doing to you also. So Samuel spoke all the*

words of the Lord to the people who had asked of him to appoint a king. And he said to them, "This will be the things that a king who reigns over you will do: **he will take your sons and place them for his desires in his chariots and among his horsemen and they will run ahead of his chariots into battle. And he will appoint for himself generals and commanders and lieutenants to command his armies. And he will make some to do his plowing and reap his harvest. And some will be forced to make his weapons of war and equipment for his chariots. He will also take your daughters for his perfumers and cooks and bakers. And he will take the best of your fields and vineyards and your olive groves and give them to those who serve him. And he will take your property and use it for his purposes. For he will take a tenth of your wealth and you yourselves shall become his property.** *Then you will cry out in that day because of your king whom you have chosen for yourselves, but the Lord will not answer you. Nevertheless the people refused to listen to Samuel and they said, "No, but there shall be a king over us, that we may be like other countries that our king may judge us and go out before us and fight our battles.*

Almost three millennia later, we still haven't learned.

MAYBE THEY CAN RE-OPEN IN GALT'S GULCH

Posted on the door of China Fun Restaurant in New York City:

> *China Fun has closed after 25 years in business. We want to thank all of our loyal customers who have been with us—whether for a day or for generations. It has been a great run serving you our delicious soup dumplings, scallion pancakes and General T'sao Chicken, but the climate for small businesses like ours in New York have become such that it's difficult to justify taking risks and running—never mind starting—a legitimate 'mom-and-pop' business. The state and municipal governments, with their punishing rules and regulations, seem to believe that we should be their cash machine to pay for all that ails us in society, even though we suffer just like everyone else from an economy in flux. Our only wish for 2017 and beyond is for our career lawmakers and politicians, local and national alike, to take a mandatory 'Undercover Boss' challenge and live in the shoes of a small business owner for a week. Maybe then they will better understand the economically stifling environment they have created, and, dare we say, change their ways for the betterment of everyone, and not just pander to the populace that garner the most votes?*

Whether it's called regulation out of existence, killing the goose that lays the golden egg, or just plain ol' stupidity, politicians and a society that believes businesses just magically grow from nothing and are forever ripe for plundering will eventually drive away the productive class, leaving nothing to take from. Ayn Rand said as much in her tome written decades ago, *Atlas Shrugged*, with a bird's-eye view of what had become her Russian homeland. It doesn't take a genius to see the same happening in 21st century Amerika.

This could only happen in a democracy when the majority of citizens believe that a business owes its very existence to the government that gives it permission to exist, provides it with roads and telecommunication lines to bring customers to its doors, and provides security forces to ensure thieves do not break in and steal its goods. This could only happen in a democracy when the majority of citizens believe that rights and privileges are bestowed upon us by our government, and so every good thing we enjoy, everything over and above a nasty, short, brutish existence we owe to our rulers.

The people fail to realize, to take into account the fact that human societies existed for thousands of generations without "benefit" of strong States. The State is that organization composed of relatively few people whose ultimate goal is control over others and who do so under threat or use of violence against those who refuse to be controlled. Humans through tens of thousands of years of of history not only existed, but thrived by developing methods of producing more than they consumed and trading their excess for the excess production of others. Some people became brokers for other's excess production. We call them business people. (Previously businessmen, but, oh well.) There is a vast body of knowledge on how humans did and could continue organizing a safe and orderly society without resorting to the wiles of a small group of men whose authority comes out of the barrel of a gun. We still manage to interact with each other and maintain a long life mostly due to social mores. This is on the decline as we turn over more and more power and authority to powerful State governments. This is, in large part, due to how we as a populace allow ourselves to be controlled through a finely-tuned propaganda machine that convinces us that without the State, those people who coral us at gunpoint, we would have no other viable options. The government education system with which the vast majority of us have been inculcated has closed off even the idea that there may be a better way.

Jesus said, "You have not because you ask not." We ask not because we imagine not. We are on a path to destruction because we have accepted lives of subservience to a class of political rulers as if this were the best of all possible worlds. The problem is not that the correct political rulers have not yet been elected to office; the problem is political rule itself.

THE BRAVE NEW WORLD

If this is the Brave New World, count me a coward. I'm glad I won't be around to see the destruction of Western society, if only the coming deluge holds out long enough.

There aren't enough of us with the courage to stand up and say some things are simply wrong. The Social Justice Warriors will win because too many of us are afraid to be called sexist, racist, cisist, misogynistic, homophobic, or whatever other -ic, -ist, or -phobic epithet comes next. We are all supposed to believe that anything and everything should be allowed, no matter the consequences to ourselves and society, all so that a miniscule minority can feel good about themselves.

This is the religion of inclusiveness.

This is the religion of tolerance.

This is the religion of non-judgmental acceptance of the rainbow of differences all around us.

Diversity is our strength!

But what the SJWs insist we throw away is the accumulated knowledge and wisdom of thousands of years of developed civilization. They cry for the jettisoning of all we've learned, not only what we call common sense, but even scientific and mathematical knowledge as if that's only a "social construct" that each individual, each generation, and society in general should be able to accept or reject as it wishes.

In ages past some science was incorrect, and, in like manner, some things we "know" to be true today will be shown to be false in the future. But that doesn't mean that we throw out the baby with the bathwater. And the SJW's use the term "social construct" as if that, by definition, is everywhere and always a bad thing. In fact, there are social constructs that have enabled the human race to sustain itself and develop over the past hundred thousand years.

What's the point? Everything is not social construct. Reality exists.

Whether one is male or female is not a social construct. There are, in fact, two sexes.

In some cases, people are born with the sexual organs of both sexes. *Both* sexes. Not all or a combination of three, four, five, or thirteen. *Both*. In days past when a baby came out of the womb with sexual organs of both sexes we would say that baby has a birth defect. The *person* is not defective, any more than someone born with a cleft palette is defective, but he or she (he or she) does have a birth defect. A Taoist saying goes, "The beginning of wisdom is calling a thing by its correct name." If a person believes himself to be multiple people depending on some unknown trigger in the brain, he has a psychological defect. If someone born with XX chromosomes believes herself to be male, by the same token, she has a psychological defect. She can have sexual relations with any live, human, willing partner over the accepted legal age, regardless of that person's chromosomal makeup. She can wear a suit and tie. She can operate a crane, drive a truck, or volunteer for the Marines and carry a gun in battle. All that notwithstanding, she is a female, a woman, graced by XX chromosomes.

However, as of 2017, I accept defeat. I accept I'm just pissing into the wind.

I've made a hobby of reading history and I can see it repeating here in the land of the previously free and home of the previously brave. There comes a time in every civilization when the strength of the people who created it atrophies into weakness, decadence, and cultural collapse as the current society settles back to enjoy the fruits of its courageous, ambitious ancestors.

Reality does not console and soften life. Reality cannot be molded to our desires. Western society prospered and grew because it developed, among other civilizing qualities, social structures. This was an event unique in the world; these social structures, conventions of civilization, applied to everyone, even the ruling class. But without fail, the blood, sweat, and tears expended by those who create a civilization eventually give way to those whose only desire, whose only ability, is to enjoy the environment that was passed to them. The generation in receipt of this gift then indulges in leisure; it can create art and spend time philosophizing. This leads to liberalism, thence to capitalism and increased individual rights. But with increasing wealth and personal freedom come greater options for personal actualization. People redirect their focus from clan and family, the building blocks of society, to themselves, seeking their own, personal benefit and growth at the expense of the social order. Eventually the society will experience declining fertility, malignant family laws, and discrimination against men and traditional values that enabled the original building of the society.

As civilized society collapses, standards of behavior and personal appearance ebb lower almost daily. History proves that after a society becomes increasingly liberal, with regards to its sexual morality, it loses its cohesion, its impetus, and its purpose. We are seeing that today, as for example, Canada's Supreme Court has adjudicated "*Most bestiality [to be] legal.*"[52]

We also know, based on history, a civilization that embraces feminist values will cease to exist. There has never been a feminist civilization that has lasted except for very short period of time, and that at the end of empire. Western men have given western women freedom of will and choice in their society. With that freedom, western women are now choosing who will take that away from them as they embrace not only liberalism, but ideologies destructive of their own self interest.[53]

Our Western society has not devolved to a point where we have embraced a new commandment, a commandment that takes precedence over all others: *Thou shalt not offend anyone, anytime, in any manner.* The poor, delicate souls who are offended then have the right to ruin said offender in their business or career, to destroy them financially, to drag them through the courts until they, as if in Mao's Red China, beat their breast and declare to the world that they are ignorant, antisocial, cowardly fools and beg forgiveness of the greater society they have insulted.

I will now step aside and watch the slow and inevitable ruin of a once-great Western Society as it is swept into the dustbin of history, thankful that I won't be around to see the ultimate collapse.

But I'll still write articles. It gives me something to do. And thankfully, I'm not the only sane person left.

---

52 http://lawnewz.com/high-profile/canadas-supreme-court-says-most-bestiality-is-legal/
53 http://www.libertyheadlines.com/feminists-embrace-islam-anti-trump-march/

MUSINGS OF A MALE OF EUROPEAN DESCENT

With reference to an article by Fred Reed at http://www.unz.com/freed/milwaukee/, I fully realize his words are somewhat harsh and he makes some points based on generalizations. (I encourage the reader to go to the address referenced above and read the entire article before proceeding. Mr. Reed makes too many cogent and intelligent points for me to adequately summarize here and I'm too lazy to ask his permission to reprint the article.) As with statistical samples, generalizations and stereotypes say absolutely nothing about a single individual, but where and when some truth lies buried in generalizations and stereotypes it shouldn't be dismissed out of hand. When truths are borne out by observation time and time again, they have a place in reasoned discussion of broad, societal issues.

Feeling uncomfortably in agreement with Mr. Reed, I find myself at a point of existential crisis as a white male in twenty-first century America. (If you'll pardon the abbreviation for *United States of America*; I know the name America comprises two continents as well as the countries of Central America. Most readers assume correctly I'm talking about U.S.A.) My discomfort stems from the difficulty of reconciling a healthy, positive sense of self with what is thrust upon me in current American culture as a White Male of European descent. Celebrations of Asian pride, Black pride, Gay pride, Pinoy Pride, La Raza, and other group identities are not only celebrated and glorified, but attendance at these celebrations has become *de rigueur* for anyone who wants to be accepted by the public and are cause for extremely positive media coverage wherever they occur.

154

But European pride? Why, that's just a synonym for White Racism. Everyone knows that. Never mind white Europeans, for the most part led by males, built the very foundations of the culture of personal liberty that allows the masses to celebrate their otherness without fear of having their tongues ripped out, their noses cut off, or being beheaded in the public square, punishments that still occur in some non-western countries. The peoples of European stock banned slavery in the West while it continued to be practiced throughout much of the rest of the world. More specifically, it was Roman Catholic priests who began the original, organized, society-wide fight against slavery and oppression of the inhabitants of the *New World*. Christian nations ended slavery centuries before it was banned in virtually every other major civilization, yet there are multitudes among us white folk who continue to flog themselves with guilt at every opportunity. With all the advances European culture has brought to the human race, still white European Christians are the only group that not only takes delight in criticizing itself but diligently does so at every opportunity in the public square. We relish to no end the crying and wailing of *mea culpas* for anyone who will listen. European civilization and its Greek and Roman predecessors are responsible for the lion's share of philosophy, art, science, and technology that brought the western world out of a life of hard labor and early death. But the more we apologize, the more we are lambasted with criticism. To unearth more insults and to find more to criticize in those of European ancestry, the Social Justice Warriors have turned to seeking out *micro aggressions*; there just aren't enough real aggressions or insults to complain about these days, so we're examined under a microscope, seeking out any and every possible word, phrase, or mode of living that could possibly be interpreted by a hyper-sensitive SJW snowflake as an insult to someone's pride.

We see now the backlash of decades of political correctness and the onslaught of Social Justice Warriors. The great unwashed masses, the mundanes in fly-over country are standing up and yelling, "I'm mad as hell, and I'm not gonna take it anymore!" A presidential candidate who is rough around the edges and is the opposite of a polished political speaker, and definitely not a schmoozer with the elites and the Wall Street crowd, has grabbed the emotions of millions upon millions who have reached the breaking point of feeling guilty and sorry and remorseful and responsible for every ill of the downtrodden classes of the country and the world. The limousine liberals, the SJW's, the poor-me crowd, those who have profited from divisiveness and especially all those who would like to see all of us of European heritage die a natural or not so natural death have sown the wind. The whirlwind draws nigh.

POST-CONSTITUTIONAL AMERICA

The citizens of the United States are living today in post-Constitutional America. There is no longer any part of that unique document that has not been willfully ignored. Precious few give a damn.

You may say you support the Constitution. If you're a government employee in a uniform you may have even sworn to uphold it. But be honest with yourself: Do you really care that that poor old piece of parchment is nothing but a historical artifact?

Do you believe the national government should force every business owner to serve every person who comes through its doors? If so, you have no use for the Constitution.

Do you believe that the national government should institute a universal health care plan for all citizens? If so, you have no use for the Constitution.

Do you believe that the national government should create laws and regulations to enforce "equal pay for equal work?" If so, you have no use for the Constitution.

Do you believe there should be a nationally-decreed minimum wage? If so, you have no use for the Constitution.

Do you believe the national government should create and enforce laws against the use of recreational drugs? If so, you have no use for the Constitution.

Do you believe that the national government should make any type of firearm illegal, or should restrict the purchase and ownership of firearms by sane, peaceful adult in any way? If so, you have no use for the Constitution.

Do you believe the president, as commander-in-chief, should send U.S. troops to seek out and kill ISIS members? If so, you have no use for the Constitution.

Do you believe "9/11 changed everything?" If so, you have no use for the Constitution.

Do you believe NSA spying is necessary to protect and defend the citizens of the United States? If so, you have no use for the Constitution.

No matter what you would like to see the national government do, to force everyone to do, or not do, if the authority for that is not stated in the supreme law of the land, *The Constitution of the United States of America*, the national government has no authority to do so.

Yes, I am well aware of the Doctrine of Implied Powers, the loose interpretations of the General Welfare Clause, and the Interstate Commerce Clause. These are simply used as pawns in games of mental and political gymnastics by the government to justify ignoring the original intent of the Constitution—to narrowly define and limit the scope of the national government.

I heard a government official say (I forget who, but I remember well the statement) that requiring every citizen to purchase health insurance was constitutional because the American people wanted universal health care—the requirement to purchase insurance was necessary to implement the will of the people. He disingenuously said that whatever the majority seems to want is constitutional. But this government bureaucrat is ignorant as sin and he's dead wrong. The Constitution was specifically intended to guard against the tyranny of the majority and the inherent problems of democracy the anti-federalists tried in vain to protect us against.

"But the restrictions of the Constitution have to have limits," you say. The Constitution is not a suicide pact. Really? What are those limits and who decides what they are? You? If you get to decide to ignore one restriction, then you have to give the same ability to a hundred million other citizens, others with whom you may violently disagree. Then where are we? The supreme law of the land contains provisions for change. If you don't like the Constitution, change it. But change it according to the rules of the game that thirteen independent states originally agreed to.

"But it's so difficult to change," you say. Of course it is. That's so people aren't able to make hasty and ill-conceived alterations. Even with those difficult impositions, mistakes have been made. Look at the eighteenth amendment. There aren't many who will defend alcohol prohibition, given the violence, lawlessness, and corruption that resulted from it, not to mention the negation of personal rights if entailed.

But now, because it's so difficult to change, we don't even try. Constitutional amendments are a relic of the past. We've forgotten our roots. We've become lazy. If the national government wants to prohibit the use of marijuana, they simply write whatever laws they want and *to hell with the Constitution*! They rest assured in the fact that the Supreme Court will go along with them, being part of the same club, the National Government. They may have to completely pervert the Necessary and Proper Clause or the Interstate Commerce Clause, but they'll find a way to shoe-horn whatever law they want into the narrow confines of the Constitution. (Miraculously, somehow, the powers that be realized that the eighteenth amendment wasn't even necessary. How foolish could they have been?)

So go ahead and force your economic mayhem on the rest of us with, as only one example, a national minimum wage law. You're so much more intelligent and compassionate than all those greedy, capitalist, exploitative business owners. You feel bad that some people don't have the intelligence or skills for which a free market would pay $15 an hour, so you want to impose laws to decree that wage. Then the next person will point out that it's impossible to raise a family in New York City on $15 an hour; the minimum should be raised to $45. It's only fair. And why not? What is so magical and perfect about $15? And if $15 an hour is good, and as long as raising the minimum wage has no impact on unemployment, as claimed by some ignorant and liberally-minded economists and political scientists, why not $100? Why not $200? Why not $1,000 an hour? Think of the economic stimulus of that much money and how much better off everyone would be!

Go ahead and force every private business owner to offer his or her services to everyone who requests them. The idea of freedom of association is long dead anyway. But please explain why someone who invested his life savings in a small business and works eighteen hours a day, 365 days a year to keep it running owes you anything.

You cannot force laws of economics to change any more than you can decree a reversal of the law of gravity. And when a KKK member comes to your bakery and requests a cake with a burning cross on it, remember that you were the one who said every business should be forced to serve every person equally, without prejudice.

Is a KKK celebratory lynching the equivalent of a lesbian marriage? No, but that's not the issue. The issue is, as a matter of principal, does a private business owner have the right to decide whom he or she does business with? Does a person have the right to decide not to purchase health insurance? Does that person have the right to purchase an insurance plan that does not include coverage for pregnancy? Does a private insurance company even have the right to offer an insurance plan that does not cover costs related to child birth? If not, why not, and who the hell are you to decide? Who gave you the moral authority to tell the rest of humanity how to act, what is acceptable, what is moral? Do you claim authority by the "social contract?" If so, show me the contract. Tell me what I have agreed to—definitively, without question or any misunderstanding, what is expected of me and what I can expect of the other parties to the contract. In case of non-compliance, what are the specific remedies available to each party of the contract? Show me my signature on the document. If you say it was decided democratically, remember that a gang rape is a democratic action. Is that really the type of society you want to live in?

The Constitution was designed to prevent the tyranny of the majority and to prevent the national government from growing into the monstrosity it has become. But don't blame politicians for that cancerous growth. The power of the national government grew one step at a time with the consent of the people. If it were not so, we would recall those who created the misguided laws and replace them with people who would follow the rules. But we like our handouts. And we like feeling protected. And we feel good thinking that everyone who wants a job is able to earn at least $30,000 a year with free health care and can take six months (or is it a year or two years?) off with pay when they decide to procreate.

So when you hear that someone is arrested and imprisoned without charge, when you hear that the police have confiscated someone's property before he is convicted or even charged with a crime, when you hear that innocent human beings have been imprisoned and tortured in a coastal prison in Cuba, when someone's home is taken under imminent domain to make way for a new shopping center, when makers of obesity-inducing high fructose corn syrup are subsidized with the help of your taxes to the tune of billions of dollars a year, when the CIA disrupts the national politics of another country and creates terrorists who fly airplanes into office buildings... Remember, you set all this in motion by demanding the national government do something unconstitutionally that you really, really believed *deep in your heart* was a good idea. But political deals are never clean, never pretty, and they ALWAYS come with unintended consequences. To give you what you want, to vote for your favorite bill, your congress critter is going to have to promise to support fifty amendments that you wouldn't touch with a ten-foot pole proposed by other congress critters and genuinely wanted deep in the hearts of their constituents (really, by their campaign donors). But that's the nature of politics. And you're willingly, if ignorantly, playing the game.

I prefer not to play the game. I'll take my chances in the market and with free-will charity and giving from the good hearts of individuals. The nature of government is to force you to do what it prescribes, or not allow you to do what it proscribes, under threat or use of violence, even to your death if you date to resist.

That's the pure and simple fact. Next time I ask someone to bake a cake for me, I'd much prefer the chance that they refuse my request, causing me to have to bid for the services of another bakery, than face the prospect that every facet of my life be determined by someone who will put me in a cage for refusing to order my life according to his dictates.

That's what the Constitution was supposed to guarantee.

One of the most inspired documents in the entire political history of mankind is dead, all so you can demand a minimum wage and force someone to bake you a cake.

John Irving Nailed It

Living in an area with too many people and cars, I spend a lot of time in mine. I can't stand commercials and useless traffic reports, and I'm too cheap to pay for a subscription service.

Fortunately, I'm alive at the most wonderful time in human history! I have Audible.com.

I recently listened to *A Prayer for Owen Meany* by John Irving recently. I enjoyed the book so much, I bought a hardback copy for my personal library—such as it is; I gave most of my hundreds of books to the Mt. Vernon, Iowa library a few years ago to lighten my load when I thought I was moving to Spain. But some books require your absolute attention and this is one of them. Listening while driving is a good way to make use of your time in awful traffic, but you miss a lot. For some odd reason, while piloting two tons of steel along an overcrowded highway, other things keep taking your mind away from the book you're listening to. You don't want to miss a single word of A Prayer for Owen Meany.

One particular page caught my attention. The book tells the life of Owen Meany from his childhood. Owen is a small person, very intelligent, seems to have some powers of discernment and knowledge of the future, and believes he is one of God's instruments on Earth. Toward the end of the book, our hero, Owen has passed through the age of innocence. Previously a rabid fan of JFK, he's found out that President Kennedy has had an affair with Marilyn Monroe and tells Johnny Wheelwright, his friend, and the story's narrator,

> *Those famous, powerful men—did they really love her? Did they take care of her? If she was ever with*

the Kennedys, they couldn't have loved her—they were just using her, they were just being careless and treating themselves to a thrill. That's what powerful men do to this country—it's a beautiful, sexy, breathless country, and powerful men use it to treat themselves to a thrill! They say they love it but they don't mean it. They say things to make themselves appear good—they make themselves appear moral. That's what I thought Kennedy was: a moralist. But he was just giving us a snow job, he was just being a good seducer. I thought he was a savior. I thought he wanted to use his power to do good. But people will say and do anything just to get the power, then they'll use the power just to get a thrill. Marilyn Monroe was always looking for the best man—maybe she wanted the man with the most integrity, maybe she wanted the man with the most ability to do good. And she was seduced, over and over again—she got fooled, she was tricked, she got used, she was used up. Just like the country. The country wants a savior. The country is a sucker for powerful men who look good. We think they're moralists and then they just use us. That's what's going to happen to you and me," said Owen Meany. "We're going to be used.

John Irving, speaking through his protagonist is right. This country is a sucker for powerful men who look good. The thing that's so difficult to fathom, though, is that we continue to allow ourselves to be played for suckers. Through every election cycle we're fed the same bullshit and we keep eating it up.

I believe we are programmed to forget unpleasantness, and the more unpleasant, the faster we forget. Maybe there's a gene that's responsible for this. I only have second-hand knowledge of the whole human procreation process, but by anyone's standards, according to anyone I've ever known who has been through the nine-month process, the entire gestation period is uncomfortable to say the least, fraught with problems or the risk of problems, and the birth process itself seems to be something no women in her right mind would go through a second time. But the human brain is programmed to forget just how awful the experience was as soon as it's over. Were it not so, the human race would have become extinct hundreds of thousands of years ago.

We also seem to have an infinite ability to believe the future is going to be better than the present. Because of this and the fact that we so easily and quickly forget the past, we believe someday we'll elect the right person and the laws of economics and human nature itself will all be changed. We'll have heaven on Earth. Maybe this unquenchable hope for the future, combined with the innate ability, and even requirement, to forget horrible moments of the past combine to keep us moving forward.

Unfortunately, we don't seem to possess much of an imagination gene. We forget the past and look to the future, but without the ability to question whether maybe we've gone down a bunny trail leading nowhere good.

I can't put my finger on exactly what's wrong, but something is and we keep looking to powerful people to lead us, to fix all that ails us, to comfort us, and to be our moral leader through all tribulation. We keep wanting what we can't have, so we keep disliking what we get.

Maybe next time we'll get it right. Until then, I'm glad I can lose myself in writing such as John Irving produces.

While we're on the topic of audible books, I have a few other thoughts I'd like to share.

I began reading The Story of Civilization by Will and Ariel Durant many years ago. I read the first volume, *Our Oriental Heritage*. (This was back when *Oriental* had not yet become the politically incorrect word it is today.) Unfortunately, I lost the set to an ex-girlfriend in a breakup. Such is life. I've recently gotten back to the series through Audible.com.

For those not familiar with this classic of the literature of history, it's a series of volumes comprising tens of thousands of pages covering virtually the entire known history of western civilization through its politics, art, and culture. No amount of writing can contain the entire history of man, but if one were to read this series and remember a quarter of the information contained within it, one would have an understanding of the origins of our western society as few others on Earth.

I don't count myself among them; I only wish I could remember ten percent of what I read, or in this case, hear. Mr. Durant covers not only the struggles among kings and emperors for control of the labor, property, and wealth of people, but the creative output of those people in literature, music, plastic arts, architecture, and everything else that becomes part of our civilization. Reading or listening to this series, one cannot help but note the incredible destructiveness of governments and individuals, acting in the name of the state, church, or simply out of their own ignorance and self-aggrandizement. The recounting of still extant information we have concerning great edifices and brilliant works of art and literature that were destroyed by this war or that battle or burned because it did not meet the narrow standards of acceptability by the person or persons in temporary power is nothing short of sickening.

I'm fully aware that nothing lasts forever; entropy and change is as much a force of nature as is creativity and growth. Beautiful buildings collapse of their own accord with age. Papyrus and paper mold and decay. Paintings fade or darken, losing their original brilliance through natural causes. Physical space is finite so the old is torn down to make way for the new.

But burning a book because it contains an idea inimical to the temporal political or religious power of the area in which it is unfortunate enough to find itself, bombing a cathedral that happens to be in the wrong place at the wrong time, destroying a beautiful sculpture because it speaks to a bourgeois mentality—this is not entropy, this is not the march of time, clearing of the old to make way for the new. This is the willful and wanton destruction of the work of millions of humans for no reason other than to promote the destroyer's desire for power and control over others.

That an incredibly small number of persons can take control of a geographical region and all the people within it with lies, deceit, false promises, violence, and even death toward those who might resist is not in and of itself the most distressing observation. That millions, even billions of people will not only accept but welcome being controlled by those few is. As noted above in the passage from First Samuel, Chapter 8, this has been the case with humankind since its earliest recorded time.

As humans, the vast majority of us want to be ruled. We want someone to take control. We want to be part of a winning team, something larger than ourselves. And we don't seem to care if the thing that's larger than we, that the winning team we're part of, is good or evil. Given our ability for self-justification, we can easily place ourselves on God's side. Our extreme emotional need to follow the leader overcomes any rational or spiritual discernment over what is acceptable behavior for a human being. When told by our leaders to shoot a person in an enemy uniform or drop a bomb on that cathedral or fly a drone to a wedding party and send a Hellfire missile into the middle of it, we simply do it. We follow orders as if we, personally, had neither accountability nor responsibility. There is no such thing as murder in warfare and governments can declare war at any time in any place, creating a limitless field of potential enemies and targets. (Today we don't even bother to declare war; we're simply at war all the time with anyone we don't like.) Then the loyal citizens, we who need to be controlled, willfully pull the trigger or push the button that destroys persons, families, and the accumulated efforts—art, architecture, literature, the accumulated written wisdom and knowledge of millions of people through history—in the blink of an eye.

WAR IS THE HEALTH OF THE STATE

If the United States government is truly "of the people, by the people, and for the people," then the people need to know what their government is doing in order to make decisions about whom they want to represent them and what they want those representatives to do in their name. I don't believe the government at this date is of, by, and for the people, but if we're to have any chance of moving toward that goal, the populace is going to have to be better informed.

Unfortunately, the national government is so complex, with so many hidden operations in every corner of the planet, and "the people" are so tied up with their own lives that it's impossible to keep up with world events that are presently affecting or will affect every one of us—not only us, but our children and grandchildren and subsequent generations. Selecting and monitoring representatives who will make decisions on matters we have delegated to them is a Sisyphean task. The national government is too large, has too much responsibility, and is run by individuals who are willing to sell their souls to have a seat at the table of power.

Randolph Bourne said, "War is the health of the state." No truer words were ever spoken. The U.S. government pursues a policy of continual war in order to thrive. It can do this only because the mainstream media have been co-opted by the government and are no more than conduits for its press releases. The financial and defense industries collude with the State and grow in direct correlation with government power, one feeding off the other and sucking the financial and psychic life blood from the general populace in order to feed the government beast. The security arms of the American State in particular have grown even faster, have become more powerful, and have become an existential threat to the well-being of not only the peoples of other countries, but of Americans themselves.

Government continues to pursue the war agenda, which perpetuates the extreme animosity directed toward the United States by the people of the countries we attempt to manipulate and control. Military experts have admitted that every "terrorist" killed creates ten more. Government policy makers know this and use it to their advantage. More terrorists means more terrorism, requiring more military and political intervention, which creates more terrorists. It's a simple, self-perpetuating cycle that naturally, seemingly organically, creates the need for more government and more oppressive security measures willingly accepted by Boobus Americanus. The size and power of the State increases, enabling the sewing of more discord and violence in every corner of the Earth, creating more "blowback" violently directed toward Americans, requiring an increase in government control and surveillance, and the cycle continues *ad infinitum*.

U.S. policymakers seem to believe that a "terrorist" is simply born that way, an aberration of nature, that there are a finite number of them and as soon as the military, the NSA, the CIA, and the FBI eradicate the last one, we'll have peace on Earth. But a terrorist is nothing more than a person who feels he is defending, with limited means, himself, his family, his culture, and his society. Just as importantly, a terrorist is one directing violence against the person using the word. Those fighting the U.S.S.R. during the 80's in Afghanistan were called Freedom Fighters by the U.S. government. When the U.S.S.R troops left and the "Freedom Fighters" turned against the United States, they were suddenly Terrorists.

The American State, taking an increasingly larger share of the peaceful, voluntary production of its citizens, can buy seemingly limitless arms and technology to wage war in every corner of the planet. Those we attack do not have an equal ability, so they improvise. They have to be creative and (dare I say it?) usually, incredibly brave. It's one thing to remotely pilot a drone into a wedding party where there *might* be a suspected terrorist (but where there are *certainly* innocent others); it's quite another to strap a bomb to yourself and look your enemy in the eye before you kill him and yourself. Is one better than the other? No, there are no betters among evil things. But I have trouble calling the remote drone pilot one of "our brave troops" in comparison with the terrorist.

We, as a people in America have no lack of any physical thing. What we lack is empathy for the millions of people on Earth who have been traumatized and suffer the results of U.S. government policy as it attempts to control the politics and economics of other nations.

Question: What does an 800-pound gorilla eat? Answer: Anything it wants. But even an 800-pound gorilla will be devoured by a hundred million mosquitoes. A minority percentage of 1.3 billion Muslims who believe in the medieval interpretation of the Qu'ran is well more than enough to continue the war against the west that justifies the constantly increasing warfare-security State. The present brute force method of warfare against them and the concomitant diminution of the liberty and quality of life the western world has created is, simply stated, not working.

For every complex problem there is a simple solution—and it is usually wrong. The solution to the Islamist problem in the world is not simple. Mohammed lived and founded a violent religion in a region of the Earth rich in oil, and to date, that oil is the major energy source of the world. The United States and other traditional western powers believe they need to control the politics and economics of Middle Eastern countries in order to ensure a constant supply of oil. The first key to resolving the problem of violence directed against the west, which our own CIA termed *blowback,* recognizing it as the result or our own actions, is to recognize and accept the fact that oil in the ground benefits no one. Those Middle Eastern countries need Western expertise and technology to convert oil from a pool of underground sludge to usable products; the people of the Middle Eastern countries are dependent upon others to develop and maintain the industry that powers their economy and provides their material lifestyle. Second, once the raw material is turned into something useful, it does the Middle Eastern countries in which it exists no good until it is sold. The people of the United States have always, barring one short period in the 70's, been able to purchase all the oil they have needed. The oil embargo of the 70's has not been repeated and most likely will not be because a cartel is an impossible arrangement to prolong for any length of time.

But the U.S. government is not so much concerned that Mr. and Mrs. Public won't have enough gas for their cars and heating oil for their home; they're concerned that they won't have the oil to power the U.S. military machine in case of war. For this there is a simple solution: eliminate the option of war. Were U.S. military forces brought back within our own shores we would have a domestic military force so strong that no nation on the face of the Earth would ever consider an attack. Even were some madman dictator to send a military force to our shores it would be repelled swiftly and easily with catastrophic results for the enemy.

With that said, peaceful free trade is still the ultimate answer to the energy needs of everyone on Earth.

There is yet one more key to the solution to the perceived problem of the risk of not having enough oil: Find another dependable source of energy. We have been reliant on oil for much too long and the businesses who control the production and supply of oil-based products have accumulated too much influence over the government. Today, were a dependable alternate method of producing electricity or of powering automobiles and trucks discovered, and that source was not controlled by the major oil companies of the world, it would never be developed or even see the light of day. Laws, rules, and regulations written by oil company lawyers and lobbyists will contain any technology that does not benefit the oil companies, and by extension, their bought and paid-for congress-critters.

The government, through its control of the mainstream media, perpetuates fear among the populace. The military-industrial interests financially benefit from the need for constant war caused by that fear, and the oil companies profit from the need for oil to power that war. Alternate sources of dependable energy would take the rug out from under those powerful organizations, but their power is so great today that this won't be allowed to happen. So we continue the cycle of attempted control and resulting violence requiring more control resulting in more violence as the energy and military interests become richer and more powerful while the rest of us suffer the loss of life and liberty.

Sadly, this will not end well. In the days before central banks and the easy creation of fiat money, governments were constrained by the real supply of wealth within their borders. Governments throughout history learned the extent of taxation that would be tolerated by the populace. To take more resulted in rebellion and eventual overthrow.

Since the creation of the central bank and the ability to create "money" out of thin air that the government "borrows" at will at interest rates manipulated for the benefit of the government and the powerful few within it, the U.S. government has been able to, at present, rack up a debt of over $18 trillion. This has only been possible by forcing interest rates below zero percent and controlling the media such that the public is led to believe that everything is still hunky dory. The laws of economics can be violated only so long before the Day of Judgment arrives. Negative interest rates, unlimited borrowing against the future, and propaganda about our "strong economy" is only a temporary solution. When the solution comes to its logical and inevitable end, the resulting economic catastrophe will annihilate the social structure of the world. Until we reach the edge of the cliff everything looks fine on the horizon. But when we reach the edge, when we get to the tipping point, the ride to the bottom will be swift and violent.

At that point, warfare will not be something we watch on the six o'clock news; it will be in our own front yard as individuals with nothing to lose scramble to take what they need to survive. We won't have to be concerned with violent Islamist terrorists when local store shelves are empty and the infrastructure of civilization we've come to rely on no longer functions. Paper money and a huge IRA in Bank of America will hold no value.

This is an unthinkable scenario, but our limitless wants and sense of entitlement, combined with an irrational and ignorant belief that government can and should provide for all our wants has led us to the point where there is no other logical outcome.

If there is a silver lining to this funnel cloud, it is that eventually the oversized, overbearing, over-powerful States of the Earth will be broken up onto smaller polities more responsible to the individual citizens and more conducive to individual liberty. A nation is a group of people with a shared culture—morals, mores, religion, and history. The attempt during modern times to force different nations, *true* nations synonymous with cultures, to live and function under an over-arching government has been a failure. We've been told that we're all human, that we all have to share this small planet, and that our strength is in diversity. We've been led to believe that the greatest social control mechanism is a violent State led by the best and brightest who have nothing but the people's best interests at heart. The truth is humans are tribal beings. The protection of our families within a manageable group, whether that is a tribe or nation, is genetically programmed. Those who rise to the top of an organization whose structure and power is maintained by threat of violence and death are not to be trusted with our welfare. Those who have any power over others must be kept under a watchful eye and on a very short leash. This can only be done if they have an extremely limited and well-defined charter under which to operate.

We have not done our duty to maintain government and accept responsibility for our own protection and sustenance. The governments of the powerful countries on Earth are out of control and will eventually collapse. The only question is when.

BIBLIOGRAPHY

Included here is a short list of books I have found to be invaluable in informing myself about the subjects of world history, philosophy, liberty, and how humans act as rational, economic beings. *A Prayer for Owen Meany* is thrown in for fun and because I enjoyed it so much.

Block, Walter. *Defending the Undefendable*. Ludwig von Mises Institute (May 1, 2008). ISBN 978-1933550176

Denson, John V. *A Century of War: Lincoln, Wilson and Roosevelt*. Ludwig Von Mises Institute; 1st edition (June 16, 2006). ISBN 978-1933550060

Healy, Gene. *The Cult of the Presidency: America's Dangerous Devotion to Executive Power* (Cato Institute, 2009) ISBN 978-1933995199

Hoppe, Hans-Hermann. *Democracy – The God That Failed: The Economics and Politics of Monarchy, Democracy and Natural Order (Perspectives on Democratic Practice)* Transaction Publishers (August 7, 2001). ISBN 978-0765800886

Irving, John. *A Prayer for Owen Meany*. William Morrow Paperbacks; Reprint edition (April 3, 2012). ISBN 978-0062204097

Kinzer, Stephen. *Overthrow: America's Century of Regime Change from Hawaii to Iraq*. Times Books; Reprint edition (February 6, 2007). ISBN 978-0805082401

Locke, John. *John Locke: 7 Works* Kindle Edition. Amazon Digital Services LLC, 2014

Locke, John. *The John Locke Collection.* CreateSpace Independent Publishing Platform (November 6, 2014). ISBN 978-1503115088

Rachels, Christopher Chase. *A Spontaneous Order: The Capitalist Case for A Stateless Society.* Jacksons - Balham, London; 1 edition (July 22, 2015). ISBN 978-1512117271

Redman, Ben Ray (editor) *The Portable Voltaire.* Penguin Classics (July 28, 1977). ISBN 978-0140150414

Rothbard, Murray N. *America's Great Depression.* Ludwig Von Mises Institute; 5th edition (June 15, 2000). ISBN 978-0945466055

Rothbard, Murray N. *Anatomy of the State.* bnpublishing.com (September 21, 2014) ISBN 978-1607967729

Woods, Thomas E., Jr. *33 Questions About American History You're Not Supposed to Ask.* Crown Forum; Reprint edition (July 22, 2008). ISBN 978-0307346698

Woods, Thomas E., Jr. *How The Catholic Church Built Western Civilization.* Regnery History, 2005. ISBN 978-0895260383

www.ingramcontent.com/pod-product-compliance
Lightning Source LLC
Chambersburg PA
CBHW071350280526
45787CB00001B/279